Parental Learning Disability
and Children's Needs

Parental Learning Disability and Children's Needs

Family Experiences and Effective Practice

Hedy Cleaver and Don Nicholson

Jessica Kingsley Publishers
London and Philadelphia

First published in 2007
by Jessica Kingsley Publishers
116 Pentonville Road
London N1 9JB, UK
and
400 Market Street, Suite 400
Philadelphia, PA 19106, USA

www.jkp.com

Library of Congress Cataloging in Publication Data
Cleaver, Hedy.
  Parental learning disability and children's needs : family experiences and effective practice /
Hedy Cleaver and Don Nicholson. -- 1st American paperback ed.
    p. cm.
  Includes bibliographical references.
  ISBN 978-1-84310-632-6 (pbk. : alk. paper) 1. Parents with disabilities--Services for--Great Britain. 2. Parents with disabilities--Family relationships--Great Britain. 3. Parents with disabilities--Government policy--Great Britain. 4. Children of parents with disabilities--Care--Great Britain. I. Nicholson, Don Thomas. II. Title.
  HQ759.912.C54 2008
  362.4085'0941--dc22
                    2007030158
British Library Cataloguing in Publication Data
A CIP catalogue record for this book is available from the British Library

ISBN 978 1 84310 632 6

Printed and bound in Great Britain by
Athenaeum Press, Gateshead, Tyne and Wear

The death of Don Nicholson in 2006 was an enormous loss to the research community and he continues to be missed by all who knew him. His career in research started in 1996, having spent a lifetime in social services working as a practitioner and senior manager in both adult and children's services. This experience gave Don the authority and confidence to negotiate successfully with chief executives and senior managers as well as the insight and sensitivity to interview anxious and confused adults. His experience of how adult and children's services work together was invaluable in helping to interpret and contextualise the findings of this study. To the research team he brought humour, tenacity and a clear headed approach. This book reflects the dedication Don gave to all his work with vulnerable children and families, and without him it would simply not have been written.

Contents

Preface

People with learning disabilities are one of the most vulnerable groups in society. This book documents the findings and conclusions of a study of children living with parents with learning disabilities. The study involved a scrutiny of social work case files and in-depth qualitative interviews carried out with a subsample of parents with learning disabilities; the children were followed up three years later to assess their progress.

The findings from this research throw light on how best to safeguard and promote the welfare of children living with parents with learning disabilities. It highlights the need for both adult and children's services to work alongside parents with learning disabilities, and stresses the importance of understanding not only the challenges many of these parents face, and how they impact on children's health and development, but also what enables some children to remain living safely with their parents. The study found no evidence to suggest that parental learning disability in itself was the reason children were removed from their parents' care.

The authors hope this book will inform the development and training of staff in all relevant disciplines and that its messages will find expression in more effective inter-agency working to improve outcomes for children and young people who are growing up in families where parents have a learning disability.

Acknowledgements

The research described in this book was done in partnership with ten local authorities and I acknowledge with sincere thanks the many people who gave generously of their time to help us identify cases, negotiate access to families and support parents with learning disabilities to feel sufficiently confident to discuss complex issues with us. I am especially indebted to the social workers and parents without whom this research would not have been possible. Parents let us into their homes, and although frequently initially confused were willing to answer our many questions as fully and as honestly as they could. Their openness in discussing subjects which were often painful and distressing helped us to understand their circumstances and experience of services. I hope that we have done justice to their accounts as they hold important messages for all those working with children who are living with parents with learning disabilities.

Of equal importance were the experiences of the service providers who were involved in this research. Despite the pressure of work that many of them were experiencing, they took time to talk to us at length. I would like to thank them all.

This study was commissioned and funded by the Department of Health (and transferred to the Department of Education and Skills). I am particularly indebted to Dr Carolyn Davies and Caroline Thomas, academic advisors to the Department of Education and Skills, who guided the research from proposal to completion.

The study benefited from the advice and support of a consultation group chaired by Carolyn Davies and Jenny Gray of the Department of Education and Skills. I would like to express my gratitude for their support and guidance. The members of this group were: Carolyn Davies, Department of Education and Skills; Jenny Gray, Department of Education and Skills; Jeff Bashton,

Previous of the Department of Health; Kevin Woods, Department of Education and Skills; Ann Gross, Department of Education and Skills; Tim Booth, University of Sheffield; Marian Moore, NCH Family Centre, Daventry; Derek Briggs, Cambridgeshire Social Services and Joseph Rowntree Trust; Jane Mason, Lincolnshire Social Services; Sue Mitchel, Lancashire Social Services.

Finally, I owe a great debt to Angela Churchill whose skills in working with adults with learning disabilities enabled us to interview parents with learning disabilities when additional help and expertise was needed. I am deeply grateful for her help.

Hedy Cleaver

Chapter 1

Introduction

In the past western society has tried to ensure that adults with learning disabilities are prevented from becoming parents. The foci of concerns have changed over time. Originally eugenic theories predominated and the aim was to ensure that offspring with similar disabilities were not born. More recently concerns have focused on the capacity of parents with learning disabilities to parent their children adequately. There has been a growing movement in the United Kingdom, however, which has questioned whether it is ethical, moral and legal to deny adults with learning disabilities the rights to live in the community, to enjoy sexual expression and to raise children.

This shift in attitudes is reflected in the government's strategy for learning disability published in 2001 which identifies four key principles at the heart of their vision to improve the lives of people with learning disability. These are: rights, independence, choice and inclusion (Cm 5086 2001). These principles are grounded in the legislation that confers rights on all citizens, including those with learning disabilities:

- the Human Rights Act 1998
- the Disability Discrimination Act 1995
- the Race Relations Act 1976
- the Race Relations (Amendment) Act 2000
- the Sex Discrimination Act 1975
- the UN Convention on the Rights of the Child, which was adopted in the UK in January 1992.

The shift in attitudes towards people with learning disabilities has led to a steady increase in the numbers of adults with learning disabilities who are parents (see, for example, Booth and Booth 1996; Dowdney and Skuse 1993; McConnell and Llewellyn 2002). Although there are no accurate data on the number of parents with learning disabilities within the population, a survey in England, in 2003–2004, of 2898 adults with learning disabilities between the ages of 16 and 91 years found 1 in 15 was a parent (Emerson *et al.* 2005).

Nonetheless, concerns over their parenting skills continue and evidence from international studies suggests that between 40 and 60 per cent of parents with learning disabilities have their children taken into care as a result of court proceedings (McConnell and Llewellyn 2002). Findings from a survey in England (Emerson *et al.* 2005) indicate a similar pattern; 48 per cent of parents with learning disabilities were not looking after their children. However, because this survey did not explore why children were not living with their parents, it should not be assumed that they had been taken into care. Discussions with one of the authors suggests a number of alternative explanations, including an agreed arrangement for relatives to care for the children, or children having grown up and left home.

Equating parental learning disability with wilful neglect and abusive parenting is *not* supported by research. There appears to be no clear relationship between intelligence – until it falls below a certain level, usually taken to be an IQ of 60 or less – and parenting (Booth and Booth 1996; Schilling *et al.* 1982; Tymchuck 1992; Tymchuck and Andron 1990).

> Of interest, is the appearance that IQ, by itself, is not a predictor either of the occurrence or of the nonoccurrence of purposeful child abuse in parents with mental retardation. (Tymchuck 1992, p.168)

Where abuse occurs it is often as a result of another person associated with the mother, such as a husband or partner (Tymchuck and Andron 1990). For example, research on child sexual abuse suggests that mothers with a learning disability are more likely to be targeted by paedophiles who gain access to children through providing practical and emotional support to the family (Cleaver and Freeman 1996).

While there is no association between parental learning disabilities and parental abuse and wilful neglect there is considerable evidence to suggest the children suffer neglect by omission as a result of a lack of parental education combined with the unavailability of supportive services (McGaw and Newman 2005). A major predictor of neglect is thought to be the degree to which the mother's resources, knowledge, skills and experiences are insufficient to meet the needs of her child (Tymchuck 1992).

The need to support parents with learning disabilities is acknowledged in the government's policy for people with learning disabilities, including those who are parents, which aims to improve their lives, through preventing prejudice and discrimination and providing sensitive and appropriate services (Cm 5086 2001).

> People with learning disabilities can be good parents and provide their children with a good start in life, but may require considerable help to do so. (Cm 5086 2001, p.81, paragraph 7.40)

Of more importance than a parent's intellectual capacity, when considering whether children are adequately cared for, are the kinds of stressors relevant to all parents. Stressors such as a large number of offspring, marital disharmony and violence, poor mental health, childhood sexual abuse, substance misuse, lack of social supports, and poverty are found to be more predictive of poor parenting than the score resulting from a standardised IQ test (Booth and Booth 1996; Dowdney and Skuse 1993). Parents with learning disabilities are particularly disadvantaged because they frequently experience a combination of these factors and are likely to be highly stressed and socially isolated (Booth and Booth 1996; Emerson et al. 2005; Feldman et al. 2002). Moreover, many of these parents have the additional challenge of caring for a disabled child: children of parents with a learning disability are at increased risk from inherited learning disabilities, psychological and physical disorders (McGaw and Newman 2005; Rende and Plomin 1993). The vulnerability of these families is acknowledged by the UK Government in their strategy for learning disability.

> Parents with learning disabilities are amongst the most socially and economically disadvantaged groups. (Cm 5086 2001, p.81)

Key to ensuring children are safeguarded and their welfare is promoted when growing up in families where parents have learning disabilities is the provision of suitable support from both informal providers, such as family and friends, and formal providers, such as voluntary and statutory agencies.

> The one feature that has consistently been shown to distinguish families where children remained at home from families where children were removed is the presence of another adult (or possibly several people) able to give support as required with matters beyond the parents' own coping resources. (Booth and Booth 1996)

Most parents with learning disabilities whose children are referred to children's social care do not have this degree of support and will require long-term, carefully co-ordinated and regularly reviewed services. The Children Act 1989 acknowledges that all parents and carers, including those with learning disabilities, need help from time to time in bringing up their children. Asking for help and advice should not be construed as a failure in parenting (HM Government 2006a).

> Parenting can be challenging. Parents themselves require and deserve support. Asking for help should be seen as a sign of responsibility rather than as a parenting failure. (HM Government 2006a, p.1, paragraph 1.4)

In particular, local authorities have a duty, under the Children Act 1989, both to safeguard and promote the welfare of children in need and wherever possible to promote the upbringing of children within their families, through the provision of services. The government defines safeguarding and promoting welfare in the following way:

> Protecting children from maltreatment; preventing impairment of children's health and development; ensuring that children are growing up in circumstances consistent with the provision of safe and effective care;…and undertaking that role so as to enable those children to have optimum life chances such that they enter adulthood successfully. (HM Government 2006b)

Services may be provided to prevent deterioration of, or maintain, or improve the child's health and development. The decision to provide services must be based on a sound assessment of the child's needs, the parents' capacity to respond to these needs, including their capacity to protect the child from significant harm, and the wider family circumstances (Department of Health, Department for Education and Employment, Home Office 2000a).

Understanding the needs of parents or carers, including those with learning disabilities, and how their needs impact on parenting capacity are integral parts of a child assessment. The subsequent plan may require services to be provided by a number of different agencies in order to support parents in safeguarding and promoting the welfare of their children, particularly in protecting them from significant harm. The Children Act 2004, and the accompanying statutory guidance on making arrangements under s11 of the Act, make it clear that safeguarding and promoting the welfare of children is central to all local authority functions and the function of all other public bodies. Effective inter-agency working and information sharing are key to its achievement (HM Government 2006a). The guidance strengthens the responsibilities of local authorities to safeguard and promote the welfare of children in need in accordance with the *Framework for the Assessment of Children in Need and their Families* (Department of Health *et al.* 2000a), and *Safeguarding*

Children (Social Services Inspectorate *et al.* 2002; Commission for Social Care Inspection *et al.* 2005).

To be successful parents and provide their children with the right start in life, adults with learning disabilities may require considerable additional help. The UK Government's *New Strategy for Learning Disability* (Cm 5086 2001) sets in place provisions to address the greater needs that people with learning disabilities experience, through offering each individual a personal Health Action Plan and ensuring that the causes of inequality are addressed.

> Strategies for improving access to education, housing and employment which enhance and promote mental wellbeing will include people with learning disabilities and mental health problems. (Cm 5086 2001, p.66, paragraph 6.25)

In addition, with the appointment of a learning difficulties tsar (Community Care 2006) and the publication of the Adult Social Care Green Paper *Independence, Well-Being and Choice* (Cm 6499) the UK Government has demonstrated a commitment to providing better information in a variety of formats to allow vulnerable adults, including those with learning disabilities, to have greater choice and control over how their needs should be met.

The Director of Adult Social Care and the Director of Children's Services will need to collaborate in order to ensure the needs of both adults and children in families are met (Cm 6499). They will need to ensure that children and adult social services teams work well together, develop a common approach and provide the required level of help.

The *Framework for the Assessment of Children in Need and their Families*, subsequently referred to as the Assessment Framework (Department of Health *et al.* 2000a), and the Integrated Children's System which builds on the Assessment Framework (Department of Health 2002) are for use with all children in need and their families, including parents with learning disabilities.

Evidence from previous work with parents with learning disabilities suggests early identification is key to the provision of well-targeted and effective services.

> Early identification of parents with learning disabilities is essential to good working practice as it enables professionals to access the appropriate specialist input and funding on behalf of their clients before major problems are encountered. (McGaw 1996, p.21)

Identifying parents with learning disabilities, however, can be hindered for a number of reasons. For example, school leavers with learning disabilities may not become registered with adult services. It may only be when a young woman with learning disabilities gives birth or returns home from hospital that her difficulties in looking after her baby become apparent. In other cases, parents with learning disabilities who are experiencing difficulties may not ask for help because they fear they will lose their child. Finally, identification may be delayed because parents who have in the past felt stigmatised by being classified as learning disabled may not seek help because they do not wish to be involved with the learning disability service.

Once concerns about children's safety and welfare have been identified, assessments should identify the strengths as well as the difficulties within children and families and take account of the parent's learning styles and capacities. In addition, assessments should include the contribution, both positive and negative, of other members of the household (such as the father or mother's partner) to the welfare of the children (McGaw and Newman 2005). In doing this staff have to guard against preconceived ideas about people with learning disabilities that may lead to identifying only evidence which supports notions of inadequacy (Tarleton, Ward and Howarth 2006) and look beyond the parents' learning disability when assessing parenting capacity (HM Government 2006a).

The challenge for local authorities is to ascertain with the family whether the child is in need and how the child and family might best be helped. The Assessment Framework was developed to support social work practitioners in carrying out assessments that result in appropriate services being provided to the child and his or her family (Department of Health *et al.* 2000a).

> A framework has been developed which provides a systematic way of ana-
> lysing, understanding and recording what is happening to children and
> young people within their families and the wider context of the community
> in which they live. (Department of Health *et al.* 2000a, p.vii)

The Assessment Framework guides practitioners when undertaking an assessment of a child to ensure the child's welfare is safeguarded and promoted by addressing:

- a child's developmental needs
- the capacity of his or her parents/carers to respond to those needs
- the impact of the wider family and environmental factors on both the child and his or her parents/carers.

The three domains of the child's developmental needs, parenting capacity, and family and environmental factors make up a framework within which practitioners can develop an understanding of what is happening to a child. In assessing the parents' capacity to meet the needs of their children, practitioners in children's social care should have access to experts with specialist skills in communicating with adults with learning disabilities and assessing the parenting capacity (HM Government 2006a). Within each of the three inter-related domains there are a number of important dimensions which practitioners are encouraged to explore when undertaking an assessment (see Figure 1.1).

The Assessment Framework was issued with practice guidance (Department of Health 2000), referral and assessment records (Department of Health and Cleaver 2000) and a set of questionnaires and scales (Department of Health, Cox and Bentovim 2000b), and was supported by training materials (NSPCC and The University of Sheffield 2000).

The findings from research on implementing the Assessment Framework suggest it has improved the quality of social work practice and increased the level of inter-agency co-operation and the degree of parental participation in the assessment process (Cleaver and Walker with Meadows 2004).

A government priority is to understand the experiences of children and their parents, where a parent has learning disabilities, when involved in a social work assessment of the children to ensure their welfare is safeguarded and promoted. To this end the then Department of Health commissioned

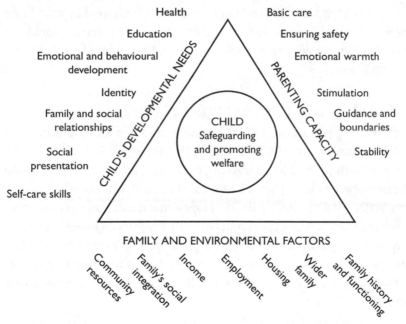

Figure 1.1 The Assessment Framework (Department of Health et al. 2000a)

Royal Holloway, University of London to undertake a study of children referred to children's social care who were living with parents with learning disabilities.

Aims and methods of the study

This research explores the needs and outcomes of children who are living with a parent with learning disabilities and are referred to children's social care. It is an empirical study carried out over six years that specifically aims to:

- explore the process of assessment for children living with a parent with learning disabilities

- identify factors that encourage or hamper the involvement of parents with learning disabilities in the assessment process

- compare the developmental needs and circumstances of children living with a parent with learning disabilities with those who do not, when referred to children's social care for similar reasons

- explore the efficacy of Child in Need Plans on outcomes for children living with a parent with learning disabilities.

The study consists of three parts. Part 1 is a study of social work case files, Part 2 is a qualitative, interview study of parents and social workers, Part 3 is a follow-up study of the children and families. The methods used in parts 1 and 2 of the research replicate an earlier study by the author that explored the impact of the Assessment Framework on all children referred to children's social care (Cleaver *et al.* 2004).

Part 1: the study of social work case files (see Chapter 2)

The case file study consists of 228 cases, drawn from ten local authorities in England. Each case refers to an individual child. The study included 76 cases where one or both parents had a learning disability and a comparison group of 152 cases where neither parent had a learning disability. Social work case files were scrutinised to identify the developmental needs and circumstances of the children. Key administrative outcomes for children included in the case file study were sought from each of the ten participating local authorities two years after the referral had been made. Outcome data were restricted to information that was expected to be electronically recorded and therefore easily accessible.

Part 2: the interview study of parents and social workers (see Chapter 3)

The interview sample of parents with learning disabilities was identified from the case file study and included 23 parents with a learning disability and the relevant social workers involved with the case. The experiences of parents with learning disabilities who had been involved in the social work assessment of their child were compared and contrasted with those of parents without a learning disability identified from an earlier study carried out by the author (Cleaver *et al.* 2004).

Part 3: the follow-up study of children living with a parent with learning disabilities (see Chapter 4)

A follow-up study was undertaken of children living with a parent with learning disabilities. Cases were included in the follow-up study when they had lived continuously, or for the majority of the time since the original assessment, with their parents. Reviews or re-assessments of children were used to explore their progress three years after the referral to children's social care.

Study methodology

A more detailed explanation of the study methods can be found in Appendix I.

Chapter 2

Referrals to Children's Social Care

This chapter is based on the information gathered from the study of social work case files. The initial part of the study of social work case files explores whether referrals involving children living with a parent with learning disabilities, referred to as *the study group* (n=76), differ from a cross-section of *all referrals*. To be included in the study group the case file had to show evidence of parental learning disability (see Appendix I for details). The second part compares the study group with a comparison group in order to identify differences and similarities between the two groups. The final part explores whether the services provided to the two groups reflect the level and degree of the child's identified needs.

The study group and a cross section of all referrals

The information on a cross section of all referrals is based on previous research by the author that involved a sample of 2248 referrals to children's social care in ten English local authorities (Cleaver *et al.* 2004).

In order to identify whether the study group differed significantly from the general population of children referred to children's social care, the following case factors were examined:

- child's principal carer
- child's age
- child's gender
- source of referral
- reason for the referral.

Child's principal carer

The sample of cases involving a parent with learning disabilities shows a similar profile, with regard to the identity of the principal carer, to all referrals to children's social care. In most cases the child's mother was the principal carer (see Table A.1, Appendix II).

Age of the children

A greater proportion of the referrals involving children living with a parent with learning disabilities were infants. For example, 47.4 per cent of children in the study group were under the age of five years compared with 34.8 per cent of all referrals. The age difference may reflect the high rates (within the range of 40% to 60%) of children removed from parents with learning disabilities (there are fewer older children living with their parents – McConnell and Llewellyn 2002) or the greater visibility that parents with learning disabilities may be under as a result of on-going contact with adult services.

Gender of the children

The proportion of boys and girls within the study group and within the sample of all referrals to children's social care were broadly similar. Boys and girls were fairly equally represented in the sample of all referrals (51.7% and 48.3% respectively) while in the study group there were slightly more boys (59.5%) than girls (40.5%).

Source of the referral

Few referrals came directly from parents with learning disabilities. The findings suggest such parents are less likely to seek the assistance of children's social care when they experience difficulties in parenting their children. In the study group a larger proportion of referrals (89.7%) came from professional sources (see Table A.2, Appendix II).

The increased prevalence of referrals from professionals may be related to the age of the children. As already noted, children living with parents with learning disabilities were more likely to be under five years. Previous research suggests that younger children are more likely to come to the attention of children's social care through professional referrals (Cleaver et al. 2004).

However, irrespective of the age of the child, parents with learning disabilities rarely sought direct help from children's social care. The interviews with parents with learning disabilities offer some insight into this anomaly.

These parents were more likely to rely on a trusted professional to make the referral to children's social care on their behalf than to make the approach themselves, as was the case with Carl's parents. (The family included baby Carl, his mother with learning disabilities, and his father with poor mental health.)

> I seemed to need help to look after the baby. I didn't think I would be able to cope. The midwife said that she would refer me and I agreed. I wanted any help I could get. (Carl's mother)

Local authority children's social care have a responsibility to 'let children and families know how to contact them and what they might expect by way of help, advice and services' (HM Government 2006a, p.79, 5.15). To enable parents with learning disabilities to approach children's social care directly for help depends on ensuring this information is in a format that takes account of their disability; accessing children's social care should be a user-friendly experience for all families. A real challenge to ensuring children living with parents with learning disabilities get the help they need is overcoming the poor experiences many parents have had of professional services (Booth and Booth 1996).

Reason for referral

In the study group (cases involving a parent with learning disabilities) the profile of why children were referred to children's social care, or a request for services made, differed from the sample of all referrals. A larger proportion of the study group were referred for 'child protection concerns', 'other parenting issues', and 'parental learning disability'. For example, in practically half the study group (46.5%) the main reason for referral was concerns about child protection, compared with approximately one-third (30.3%) of all referrals to children's social care. The increased rate of child protection concerns should not be seen as synonymous with abuse and wilful neglect; previous research indicates that concerns are likely to arise because parents fail to address their children's needs, i.e. neglect through omission (Schilling *et al.* 1982; Seagull and Scheurer 1986; Tymchuck and Andron 1990; Tymchuck 1992).

In one-fifth of the study group the referral related to other parenting issues (21.1%), yet this was a reason for only 15.4 per cent of all referrals, or it related to parental learning disability (19.7%), an issue understandably rarely relevant in the sample of all referrals.

While these issues were over-represented, others were under-represented. For example, parental mental illness and substance misuse rarely featured as the primary reason for referral in the study group, and in only one case was the behaviour of a young person the main reason for referral. This divergence may reflect the smaller proportion of (a) older children and (b) referrals from parents and relatives in the study group. Both these issues are associated with parental requests for services (Cleaver *et al.* 2004).

Discussions with social workers and professionals in relevant agencies indicate that the parent's learning disability – the primary reason for referral in one-fifth (19.7%) of cases – may overshadow other concerns within the family when a referral is made to children's social care. This suggests that the two prejudicial presumptions about parents with learning disabilities discussed by McConnell and Llewellyn (2002) may continue to affect practice.

> The first of these is that these parents will inevitably maltreat their children or put them at risk from others. The second presumption is that any perceived parenting deficiencies (or risks to the child) are irremediable and that there is therefore little point in offering such parents supports. (McConnell and Llewellyn 2002, p.302)

Identifying the comparison group

In order to explore the similarities and differences between cases involving parents with learning disabilities from similar cases where parents did not have learning disabilities, a comparison group was identified from the sample of 2248 referrals featured in the author's previous study (Cleaver *et al.* 2004). The following criteria were used to identify the comparison group:

- the reason for the referral
- the age group of the child
- the gender of the child
- the local authority responsible for the case.

In cases where the parent's learning disability had been cited as the main reason for the referral (n=14) case matching had to be based on the remaining criteria: age group of the child, gender of the child, and the local authority responsible for the case.

The study group and a comparison group
Referrals

The sample consisted of 228 referrals made up of 76 cases that involved children living with a parent with learning disabilities (*the study group*) and a *comparison group* of 152 cases where children lived with parents without learning disabilities (see Appendix I for details).

Referrals of children living with a parent with learning disabilities were only slightly more likely to be re-referrals to children's social care than referrals involving parents who did not have learning disabilities.

> A re-referral is defined as a referral about the same child/young person within a twelve month period from when the child's case was last closed. (Department of Health 2000, p.2)

Information on re-referrals was available on 45 cases in the study group. For 16 of these cases (35.6%), the social worker had recorded the referral as a re-referral – a slightly larger proportion than that found for the comparison group (21.4%).

PARENTAL AWARENESS OF THE REFERRAL

Professionals were just as likely to inform parents with learning disabilities of their intention to refer their child to children's social care as they were in cases where parents did not have learning disabilities. Social workers had recorded that parents were aware of the referral in 71.7 per cent of cases involving a parent with learning disabilities compared with 72.8 per cent of cases in the comparison group.

ACTION ARISING FROM THE REFERRAL

The referral form issued with the Assessment Framework (Department of Health and Cleaver 2000), and used as the blueprint for the Integrated Children's System electronic records, includes a section for social workers to record the decision made following the referral or request for services (Department for Education and Skills 2006). Social workers can record the following decisions:

- information to be provided to the family
- referral to another agency
- progress to an initial assessment
- some other action
- no further action.

An exploration of this information shows the action arising from the referral differed between the study group and the comparison group in two aspects:

- In the sample where children were living with a parent with learning disabilities, social workers were *more* likely (noted in 56 cases, 73.7%) to progress the case to an initial assessment than in the comparison group (noted in 76 cases, 50%).

- Social workers were *less* likely to take no further action (noted in 6 cases, 7.9%) in the sample where children were living with a parent with learning disabilities than in the comparison group (noted in 52 cases, 34.2%).

There was little difference in the proportion of cases where information was provided to the family, or where the family was referred to another agency.

These findings must, however, be treated with caution and may be biased because the method used to identify 59 of the 76 cases in the study group required some documentation being available on the case file; most of these cases progressed on from the referral (see Appendix I for details). Nonetheless, discussions with social work practitioners and managers suggest that referrals, where the parent has been identified as having learning disabilities, generally result in some form of action being taken and the findings reflect this social work practice.

The difference between the two groups in relation to the proportion of referrals that led to some form of assessment is even greater if both initial and core assessments are considered. In only 10.5 per cent of cases where children were living with a parent with learning disabilities did the referral *not* lead to some form of assessment. In contrast practically half the referrals (43.4%) in the comparison group did not progress to either an initial or core assessment.

Initial assessments

An initial assessment is defined as a brief assessment of each child referred to social services with a request for services to be provided. This should be undertaken within a maximum of 7 working days but could be very brief depending on the child's circumstances. It should address the dimensions of the Assessment Framework, determining whether the child is in need, the nature of any services required, from where and within what timescales, and whether a further, more detailed core assessment should be undertaken. (Department of Health *et al.* 2000a, p.31, paragraph 3.9)

In 132 cases the referral progressed to an initial assessment, evidenced by a completed Initial Assessment Record on the case file (see Department of Health and Cleaver 2000 for an explanation of the records). This was made up of 56 cases where children lived with a parent with learning disabilities and

76 cases where children lived with parents who did not have learning disabilities.

NUMBER OF AGENCIES INVOLVED IN THE INITIAL ASSESSMENT

To ensure families that include a parent with learning disabilities receive comprehensive services depends on inter-agency co-operation during assessment, planning, intervention and review. The study found a similar number of agencies were involved in the initial assessment regardless of whether the children were or were not living with a parent with learning disabilities. For example, three or more agencies were involved in approximately one-third of initial assessments in both the study group (30.3%) and the comparison group (29.3%). However, the interviews with social workers suggest learning disability teams within adult services are not routinely involved at this stage.

REASONS FOR THE INITIAL ASSESSMENT

Because the reason for referral was one of the criteria used in matching the study group and comparison group, the profile for why initial assessments had been undertaken should be broadly similar for the two groups. Previous research shows that the reason for the initial assessment reflects the reason for the referral (Cleaver et al. 2004).

The findings (see Table A.3, Appendix II) show considerable similarities between the two groups. Child protection concerns were the primary reason for the initial assessment in both the study group (accounting for 42.6% of initial assessments) and the comparison group (accounting for 48.6% of initial assessments). The child's disability accounted for a small proportion of initial assessments in both groups (5.6% in the study group and 2.8% in the comparison group).

However, a number of factors did differentiate the two groups. Some were expected and reflected the reason for the referral, such as parental learning disability, which accounted for 16.7 per cent of initial assessments in the study group but did not feature in the comparison group. Others had not been anticipated. For example, in cases where parents had learning disabilities, social workers were more likely to record the primary reason for the initial assessment in terms of non-specific concerns about parenting capacity (noted in 25.9% of cases). Such non-specific concerns accounted for only 16.7 per cent of initial assessments in the comparison group. Finally, social workers rarely (7.4%) recorded domestic violence, parental drug and alcohol misuse, and parental mental illness as primary reasons for an initial assessment in the study group, but these were issues that accounted for 19.4 per cent of initial assessments in the comparison group.

FINDINGS FROM THE INITIAL ASSESSMENT

In carrying out an initial assessment the practitioner will explore each of the dimensions that relate to the child's development, parenting capacity, and family and environmental factors (for details see Figure 1.1, Chapter 1). In assessing whether a child has developmental needs, practitioners should gather information from a variety of sources, including scales and questionnaires where relevant. For example, in finding out about a child's health the practitioner should consult his or her own agency's records, see and talk to the child or young person where appropriate, talk to the child's parents, and consult with health and other relevant professionals.

The child's developmental needs

The pattern of children's developmental needs, identified in both the study group and comparison group, reflects that found in previous research (Cleaver *et al.* 2004). Social workers identified the greatest level of developmental need in relation to children's family and social relationships, and fewest needs in relation to children's identity. For example, over three-quarters of children living with parents with learning disabilities had developmental needs in relation to their family and social relationships, approximately 60 per cent in relation to health and education, and half the group had needs in relation to their emotional and behavioural development (see Table A.4, Appendix II).

Although the overall profile of the child's developmental needs was similar for both the study group and comparison group, a greater proportion of children in the study group had identified developmental needs with regard to every dimension (see Table A.4, Appendix II).

Cases were classified as having severe needs when social workers recorded that the child had developmental needs in three or more of the five developmental dimensions (Cleaver *et al.* 2004). An analysis of the study group (children living with a parent with learning disabilities) and the comparison group (children not living with a parent with learning disabilities) shows significant differences (Pearson Chi-square 4.760 (1) <.029). Over half the children (51.8%) in the study group were classified as having severe developmental needs, whereas only one-third of children (32.9%) in the comparison group met these criteria.

Parenting capacity

The profile of the study group and comparison group differed in relation to the parent's capacity to meet the needs of their children. The comparison group mirrored previous research findings (Cleaver *et al.* 2004) where parenting was causing most concern in relation to parents' capacity to ensure their child's safety, and the capacity to provide stability for their children. The profile of the study group, however, showed a rather different pattern. Except for 'emotional warmth' (and even this proportion was higher than the comparison group), there was a high rate of difficulties recorded for every parenting dimension (see Table A.5, Appendix II). For example, approximately half the group of the parents with learning disabilities experienced difficulties in providing basic care (54%), ensuring safety (58%), providing adequate stimulation (56.3%), providing adequate guidance and boundaries (68.1%), or providing the stability their children needed (47.9%).

The research team classified cases as having severe parenting difficulties when social workers had recorded parenting difficulties in three or more of the six dimensions. A significant proportion of cases in the study group were classified as having severe parenting difficulties (Pearson Chi-square 7.727 (1) <.005). Over half (57%) the cases in the study group were classified as having severe parenting difficulties compared with one-third (32.9%) of the comparison group.

Family and environmental factors

Social workers recorded a greater rate of problems in relation to the domain of 'family and environmental factors' in both the study group and comparison group than for either children's developmental needs, or parenting capacity, reflecting the findings from previous research (Cleaver *et al.* 2004). The chief cause for concern was 'family history and functioning'.

Although the profiles for both groups were similar, once again a much greater proportion of children and their families in the study group experienced difficulties for every one of the family and environmental factors (see Table A.6, Appendix II). For example, 89.4 per cent of these families were experiencing difficulties in relation to family history and functioning, two-thirds in relation to social resources, and approximately one-half in relation to employment.

A significantly greater proportion of cases within the study group was classified as having severe difficulties in relation to family and environmental factors (two or more factors identified as not being adequate: Pearson

Chi-square 6.641 (1) <.010). In practically two-thirds (66.1%) of cases in the study group, children and families were experiencing severe difficulties in relation to family and environmental factors compared with 43.4 per cent of those in the comparison group.

The following notes, recorded on the Initial Assessment Record, introduce the Tandy family who were experiencing severe difficulties in relation to their home conditions. The family comprised both parents and their four children: Janice (eight years), Pamela (seven years), Emma (four years) and Adam (two years) and their parents, Charles and Catherine. To ensure the anonymity of families, all names have been changed.

> Home visit 1. Charles had been drinking and the home conditions weren't improving at all. Adam looked dirty and poorly. I asked Charles to pick up the dog excrement from the garden as the children were playing in it. Again asked them to start making some improvement to the children's rooms.

> Home visit 2. No improvement in home conditions. Charles had been drinking. Catherine had also had a birthday drink.

Multiple problem cases

Cases were classified as having multiple problems when the initial assessment identified severe difficulties in all three domains: children's development *and* parenting capacity *and* family and environmental factors. In a previous large study of referrals, multiple problem cases accounted for seven per cent of initial assessments (Cleaver *et al.* 2004).

The initial assessment showed that in the current study 25 children (19%) met these criteria. However, children living with a parent with learning disabilities were significantly more vulnerable (Pearson Chi-square 14.234 (1) <.000). One-third (33.9%) of the study group was classified as experiencing multiple problems compared with 7.9 per cent of the comparison group. These findings support previous studies that highlight the considerable adversity faced by parents with learning disabilities.

> Shortage of money, debt, unemployment, chronic housing problems, fraught relationships, the hardships of single parenthood, personal harassment, victimisation and skill deficits all contribute to their vulnerability. (Booth and Booth 1996, p.15)

Although practically two-thirds of children living with parents with learning disabilities were not classed as having multiple problems, nonetheless only six children (10.7%) were found *not* to have severe needs in at least one of the three domains. This finding suggests that in most cases a careful core assessment would be needed to establish the most appropriate intervention. The rate of children *not* having severe needs in any domain was higher in the comparison group; practically one-third (31.6%) of the group were not rated as having severe needs in any domain.

DECISIONS RECORDED ON THE INITIAL ASSESSMENT RECORD

The guidance issued with the assessment records (Department of Health 2000) informs social workers that the *Further action* section should be used to record any action taken during, or on completion of, the initial assessment. The Initial Assessment Record allows social workers to record more than one action when it is appropriate. Social workers did not always record the action to be taken, reflecting findings from previous research (Cleaver *et al.* 2004), and as a result the findings should be treated with some caution. In fact, discussions with social workers revealed that it is not uncommon for considerable work to be undertaken with a child and family which is not detailed on the case record.

The study group showed both similarities and differences to the comparison group in relation to the decisions recorded on the Initial Assessment Record. Similarities related to the proportion of cases referred to another agency, referred for legal action, or where no further action was the recorded decision. For example, there was no significant difference in relation to the proportion of cases referred to another agency. This applied to 57.9 per cent of cases (n=22) in the study and 38.7 per cent (n=24) of cases in the comparison group (information was missing for 18 cases in the study group and 14 cases in the comparison group). In neither group was a case referred for immediate legal action.

Social workers rarely recorded 'no further action' as the decision in cases involving children living with a parent with learning disabilities. Although this was the recorded decision in over one-third of cases (39.7%) in the comparison group, it had only been noted in two cases (4.3%) in the study group (information was missing for 10 cases in the study group and 13 cases in the comparison group).

In contrast, social workers were more likely to record a decision either to provide services to children and their families, or to ensure that a core assessment was carried out. A decision to provide services to the child and family was noted in 73.2 per cent (n=30) of cases in the study group and 43.5 per cent (n=27) of cases in the comparison group (information was missing for 15 cases in the study group and 14 cases in the comparison group). Similarly, a core assessment was the recorded decision in 32.4 per cent (n=11) of cases in the study group, but noted on only one child's case record in the comparison group (information was missing for 22 cases in the study group and 14 cases in the comparison group).

In three cases in the study group social workers had recorded that a strategy discussion was to be held because of concerns about possible significant harm to the children, a decision noted in one case in the comparison group.

In multiple problem cases social workers were significantly more likely to record that the case was to proceed to a core assessment. This was the recorded decision in 8 of the 25 multiple problem cases compared with only 9 of the 107 cases not classified as multiple problem cases. Nonetheless, in two-thirds (68%) of the multiple problem cases the recorded decision was *not* to carry out a core assessment.

THE PROVISION OF INFORMATION TO FAMILIES

When the case involved a parent with learning disabilities, social workers were less likely to provide families with a copy of the Initial Assessment Record. A copy was given to about one-tenth (n=6) of families where a parent had learning disabilities compared with one-fifth (n=16) of families in the comparison group. Not providing a copy of the Initial Assessment Record to families where parents have learning disabilities may be an appropriate decision. However, parents with learning disabilities should be provided with a record of the initial assessment and the decisions taken in a format and style that takes account of their disability and learning styles.

Core assessments

A core assessment is deemed to have commenced at the point the initial assessment ended, or a strategy discussion decided to initiate enquiries under s47, or new information obtained on an open case indicates a core assessment should be undertaken. (Department of Health *et al.* 2000a, p.32, paragraph 3.13)

The record of a core assessment was found on the case files of 40 cases (see Department of Health and Cleaver 2000 for an explanation of the records).

INCONSISTENCIES BETWEEN DECISIONS RECORDED ON THE INITIAL ASSESSMENT
RECORD AND DOCUMENTATION FOUND ON THE CASE FILE

There was considerable inconsistency between the decisions recorded on the
Initial Assessment Records and the documentation found on the case files, a
finding that mirrors previous research (Cleaver *et al.* 2004). Such inconsistencies were found for both the study group and the comparison group.

Core Assessment Records were found on the case files of 33 cases where
this had *not* been the decision recorded on the Initial Assessment Record.
These resulted from:

- 11 cases where the social worker had not recorded the outcome of
  the assessment on the Initial Assessment Record
- 2 cases where the recorded decision had been *not* to proceed to a
  core assessment
- 20 cases where no initial assessment had been carried out, and
  referrals simply progressed to core assessments.

In 10 cases the decision recorded on the Initial Assessment Record had been
to carry out a core assessment, but no Core Assessment Record was found on
the case file. In none of the four cases where a strategy discussion had been
recorded was there a core assessment on the case file. In every case the
recorded decision was to initiate s47 enquiries. Government guidance is clear
that a core assessment is the means by which these enquiries should be carried
out (HM Government 2006c).

POSSIBLE REASONS FOR THE MISMATCH

Inconsistencies between the decisions recorded on the Initial Assessment
Record and the documentation found on the case file may result from a variety
of factors.

Good practice

The findings suggest that in some cases the inconsistency was the result of
good practice. For example, a detailed scrutiny of the data reveals ten
instances where new information on an open case triggered a core assessment.

Family is well known to adult social services

Some (n=21) of the families in the study group had been referred from
adult social services. In six cases social workers initiated a core assessment

immediately on receiving the referral. The decision to carry out a core assessment was based on the information given by adult services.

A core assessment carried out on a single child in a sibling group

There was some evidence that in large sibling groups social workers carried out core assessments on a selected child, often the youngest. For example, in one case where there were eight siblings, the decision to initiate a core assessment had been recorded on the Initial Assessment Record for each child. However, evidence of a core assessment was found on the case files of only two of the children. The same practice was found in two further large sibling groups. For the other children in the family some information about their health and development was to be found on the running record. Information about parenting capacity, and family and environmental factors was assumed to be common to all the siblings. There was no evidence in the case record of an analysis that took account of the differential effect of these issues on the developmental needs of individual children. Concentrating on a single child in the family may be understandable given the pressures on social workers, but such practice is unsafe. Assessments should be child focused not family focused, and account taken of the individual child's needs, in particular how they are parented and how the wider family and environment are affecting them personally.

Dual assessment and recording systems

The structure of some children's social care departments meant that separate assessment procedures operated for cases when (a) enquiries were made under s47 of the Children Act 1989 and/or when (b) the children were disabled.

Enquiries under s47

When the decision is to initiate s47 enquiries, Government Guidance – *What to Do if You're Worried a Child is Being Abused* (HM Government 2006c) and *Working Together to Safeguard Children* (HM Government 2006a) – are clear that as a consequence a core assessment should be commenced, or, where one is already in progress, completed.

The study found social work practice was not always in line with government guidance. For example, among the study group (children living with a parent with learning disabilities) in seven cases a strategy discussion took place that resulted in enquiries being initiated under s47. In no case was a

Core Assessment Record found on the case file. As a result of these enquires the names of six children were placed on the Child Protection Register. The findings suggest that the report made to the child protection conference (for sibling groups this was a joint report), evaluating the risk of significant harm to the child(ren), took the place of the core assessment. Government guidance is clear that information gained from the initial and core assessments should be used to inform the report made to the initial child protection conference.

> LA children's social care should provide the conference with a written report that summarises and analyses the information obtained in the course of the initial assessment and the core assessment undertaken under s47 of the Children Act 1989 (in as far as it has been completed within the available time period) and information in existing records relating to the child and family. (HM Government 2006a, p.100, paragraph 5.89)

Disabled children

Twelve referrals involved a disabled child. In only one case did the social worker carry out both an initial and a core assessment. The type of assessment differed not only in relation to the identified needs of the child, but also in relation to the culture of the local authority. For example, in some cases (n=6) there appeared to be a culture of passing cases to the 'children with disabilities team' once an initial assessment had been completed. Children were then assessed in relation to whether they met the threshold for the provision of a particular service. No Core Assessment Record was found on the case file. In other cases (n=4) the families were well known to children's social care and referrals led directly to a core assessment.

The following case is an example of decision-making that did not appear to be based on an assessment of the children's needs. A referral to children's social care in relation to a case open to adult services (mother with learning disabilities) concerned the mother's alcohol problems and the welfare of her two children. This family had a long history of child protection concerns, registration and periods of accommodation for the children. The daughter of 14 years had learning disabilities, although her nine-year-old brother did not. It was noted on the case files of both children that a 'pre-assessment', including an initial visit to the home, had been made. On the basis of this no further action was undertaken in relation to the girl, although a strategy discussion resulted in enquiries under s47 being initiated in relation to the boy. No initial or core assessment was undertaken for either child. It was therefore not clear on what information decisions taken about each child were based.

Cases that progressed to a core assessment

Core assessments were carried out in 40 cases and were significantly more likely to be carried out in cases where the child was living with a parent with learning disabilities. In 26 cases (34.2%) in the study group a core assessment was carried out, compared with 14 cases (9.2%) in the comparison group.

THE INVOLVEMENT OF PARENTS

The study of the Core Assessment Records suggests that parents in the study group were rarely provided with information about their rights. For example, in only three of the 26 cases was it recorded on the Core Assessment Record that a parent with learning disabilities had been given a copy of the social services department's complaints procedures or information about access to records. The Records suggest such information was provided in 6 of the 14 cases where parents did not have learning disabilities.

At the time of the study the participating local authorities had not produced this information in an accessible format for people with learning disabilities using, for example, Makaton or Easy English, tape or CD rom. In some cases social workers may have discussed these issues with parents with learning disabilities rather than handing over inaccessible written material. However, research suggests that disabled parents experience great difficulty in getting information (Morris 2003). Parents with learning disabilities need information in an accessible format that explains their service entitlements, and informs and reassures them. This information should be widely distributed in places that parents with learning disabilities go (Wates 2002).

In contrast social workers were more likely to record the views of parents with learning disabilities on the Core Assessment Record. This had been done in just over one-fifth of cases (n= 6) in the study group but was not found in any case in the comparison group. This finding may reflect poor recording practice and it would be unsafe to assume that, where this information had not been recorded on the Core Assessment Record, parents' views had not been sought.

THE INVOLVEMENT OF OTHER AGENCIES IN THE ASSESSMENT

In the majority of cases agencies working with children, such as health and educational services, contributed or were involved in the core assessment (health involved in 70% and education in 60% of core assessments). In contrast, learning disability teams within adult services were rarely involved unless they were working with the parents. This lack of involvement reinforces findings from the interviews with social workers and reflects the initial assessments.

> Assessing parenting capacity when a parent has learning disabilities needs to address: a parent's capacity and motivation to acquire new skills; their potential to mainstream and generalise newly acquired skills; and their ability to keep abreast of their child's developmental needs. (McGaw 1996, p.24)

The evidence from inspections suggests that where specialist assessments have not been carried out and/or learning disability support services have not been involved, crucial decisions may be made on inadequate information (HM Government 2006a).

QUESTIONNAIRES AND SCALES AND SPECIALIST ASSESSMENTS

To help social workers in assessing children and families a pack of questionnaires and scales was published to accompany the Assessment Framework (Department of Health *et al.* 2000b). The pack includes the following eight instruments:

1. *The Strengths and Difficulties Questionnaire* screens for emotional and behavioural problems in children and adolescents.
2. *The Parenting Daily Hassles Scale* assesses the frequency and intensity of daily 'hassles' experienced by adults caring for children.
3. *The Home Conditions Scale* addresses various aspects of the home environment.
4. *The Adult Wellbeing Scale* explores an adult's feelings of depression, anxiety and irritability.
5. *The Adolescent Wellbeing Scale* provides insight into how an adolescent feels about his or her life.
6. *The Recent Life Events Questionnaire* explores the impact on families of recent life events.
7. *The Family Activity Scale* identifies the type of environment provided to the children through exploring the kinds of activities the family members engage in.
8. *The Alcohol Scale* helps identify alcohol disorders and hazardous drinking habits.

The study of social work case files suggests that social workers rarely use these questionnaires and scales when carrying out core assessments. Evidence of their use was found in four cases (two in the study group and two in the comparison group). For example, in the two cases involving parents with learning disabilities, social workers had used the following set of scales and questionnaires: 'The Parenting Daily Hassles Scales', 'The Adult Wellbeing Scale', and 'The Alcohol Scale'. Social workers had used the following for the two cases in the comparison group: 'The Recent Life Events Questionnaire', 'The Alcohol Scale' and 'The Home Conditions Scale'. Although many families where parents had learning disabilities were living in very poor conditions, it is of some concern that 'The Home Conditions Scale' (designed to explore the impact of the home on children's wellbeing) was not used. Interviews with social workers suggest that a lack of familiarity with, and training in relation to, these questionnaires and scales meant social workers were unsure of their benefits (Cleaver *et al.* 2004).

No differences were found between the two groups with regard to the commissioning of specialist assessments to inform the core assessment. In 5 of the 26 cases (19.2%) where the child lived with a parent with learning disabilities a specialist assessment, carried out at a family centre, was commissioned, compared with 3 of the 14 cases (21.4%) in the comparison group. However, family centre workers may not always have the expertise to assess parenting skills when parents have learning disabilities. McGaw and Newman (2005) provide a helpful review of assessments of parenting capacity for use with parents with learning disabilities.

TIME TAKEN TO CARRY OUT THE CORE ASSESSMENT

The interviews with social workers and notes on case files suggest practitioners experience difficulties in completing core assessments within the required time when parents have learning disabilities.

> The need to assess the parenting skills and mother's disabilities will mean this is not going to be done within the required 35 days. (Noted by a social worker on a Core Assessment Record)

It proved difficult to establish how long social workers had taken to complete core assessments because they had not always recorded the end date of the assessment on the Core Assessment Record. This had been noted in only 18 of the 37 cases (13 cases in the study group and 5 cases in the comparison group).

Because the numbers in the comparison group are small, the findings for the study group have been compared with the findings from previous research by the author (Cleaver *et al.* 2004). This comparison shows that a smaller proportion of core assessments that involved parents with learning disabilities were completed within the required time. In 53.5 per cent (n=7) of cases in the study group the assessment was completed on time compared with 73.5 per cent in previous research (Cleaver *et al.* 2004).

To calculate the completion rate based on cases where the end date had been recorded may be misleading, as a failure to record this may indicate the assessment had over-run. If it is assumed that assessments that lacked a recorded end date took longer than the required 35 days, the disparity was still evident. Approximately one-quarter (26.9%) of assessments in the study group (parents with learning disabilities) were done on time compared with over one-third (36.2%) in the previous research (Cleaver *et al.* 2004).

These findings are based on very small numbers and must be treated with caution. Nonetheless, they support the reports of social workers who expressed concerns that assessments involving parents with learning disabilities required more time (discussed in Chapter 3).

FINDINGS FROM THE CORE ASSESSMENT

The core assessment is an in-depth assessment that explores all the dimensions that relate to the child's development, parenting capacity, and family and environmental factors (for details see Figure 1.1, Chapter 1). It should build on the findings of any current initial assessment and take account of historical data both in terms of any previous concerns relating to the child, or other children within the family, and the parents' own background. To gain a holistic understanding of the needs of children living with parents with learning disabilities will require consultation with partner agencies and adult services.

Children's developmental needs

The core assessments identified high levels of developmental needs in both the study and comparison group. Because the numbers are small, Table A.7 (Appendix II) compares the study group (parent with learning disabilities) with both the comparison group and previous research by the author (Cleaver *et al.* 2004). The findings show that social workers carrying out core assessments on children living with a parent with learning disabilities identified higher levels of developmental needs in practically every dimension, reflecting the results of the initial assessment. Children in the study group were particularly disadvantaged in relation to their 'family and social relationships', 'social presentation', and 'selfcare skills'.

Parenting capacity

The Core Assessment Records identify a greater proportion of parents in the study group having difficulties in parenting their children, once again reflecting the findings from the initial assessments. In 75 per cent of cases in the study group parents were recorded as experiencing difficulties compared with two-thirds (66.6%) of cases in the comparison group (the latter figure mirrors the rate found in previous research, Cleaver *et al.* 2004).

A number of issues have been shown to impair parents' capacity to respond appropriately to the needs of the children. The Core Assessment Record enables social workers to record the presence of issues such as parental physical or mental illness, parental drug misuse, domestic violence, a history of childhood abuse, or growing up in care (Cleaver, Unell and Aldgate 1999).

Information was available in 23 of the 26 cases in the study group and 9 of the 14 cases in the comparison group. The data show that all but one of the parents (95.7%) with learning disabilities were also experiencing one or more additional issue that affected their parenting. This is somewhat greater than the proportion found in the comparison group (77.8%). For example, in the study group seven mothers with learning disabilities had been in care during their own childhood, six parents were survivors of childhood abuse, ten had a history of violence, and ten were substance misusers. This prevalence of co-morbidity for parents with learning disabilities has been identified in previous research (Cotson *et al.* 2001; McConnell and Llewellyn 2000).

The recording on the Core Assessment Record in the following case illustrates the extent of co-morbidity in some families.

> Mum describes herself as having a series of difficult life experiences. She reports experiencing domestic violence in all her relationships and has a variety of physical health problems and has intermittent chronic depression, specific learning disabilities and agoraphobia. A family history of both learning difficulties and mental health problems exists.

Family and environmental factors

Once again the findings from the core assessment reflect those from the initial assessment: a larger proportion of children and families in the study group were experiencing difficulties in relation to family and environmental factors. Three-quarters of families in the study group were recorded as being disadvantaged because of their family and environmental factors, compared with half (50%) of the comparison group.

These findings support the interviews with social workers (to be discussed in the next chapter) that reveal the poverty and inadequate living conditions many children living with a parent with learning disabilities grow up in. Research suggests that poverty is a risk factor for families and has a negative impact on parenting (Ghate and Hazel 2002).

Parents with learning disabilities may experience problems over finance and housing because they find it difficult to access their entitlements to support under the community care legislation (Morris 2003). Moreover, relatively few people with learning disabilities receive direct payments, which are an important way to have choice and control over the assistance they need, although some local authorities are taking steps to increase take-up (Cope 2003). A further relevant factor is a benefit system which recognises the additional costs of parenting a disabled child but does not acknowledge the additional expenditure families may incur due to a parent being disabled (Morris 2003).

MULTIPLE PROBLEM CASES AT CORE ASSESSMENT

A comparison of the study and comparison groups shows that a higher proportion of families in the study group were rated by the researchers as experiencing multiple problems, that is severe difficulties in all three domains. The Core Assessment Record suggests that every family in the study group experienced severe difficulties in at least two domains and that in 83.3 per cent of cases severe difficulties were identified in all three domains. In the comparison group 55.6 per cent of cases were rated as having severe needs in all three domains.

PLANS ARISING FROM CORE ASSESSMENTS

The core assessment should result in a Child in Need Plan. The information gathered during the core assessment forms the baseline about the child's developmental needs, parenting capacity and family and environmental factors. An analysis of these findings will provide an understanding of the child's circumstances and should inform planning, case objectives and the nature of service provision. The Child in Need Plans should show specific and concrete areas for change, how services are expected to achieve the planned outcomes for the child or support the changes, and in what timescale.

Core assessments carried out with children in the study group were more likely to result in a Child in Need Plan than for children in the comparison group. In over two-thirds of cases (n=18, 69.2%) in the study group there was a Child in Need Plan, compared with 28.6 per cent (n=4) cases in the comparison group. In the author's earlier study, plans were found in one-third of cases (Cleaver *et al.* 2004).

For the study group every Child in Need Plan addressed the parenting issues. Fourteen of the 18 plans addressed the child's developmental needs and in 15 cases the plan covered family and environmental factors.

Administrative outcomes

Administrative information about the services provided to children and families during the two years following the assessment was sought on the study group and half the comparison group. The local authorities were able to provide data in relation to approximately three-quarters (76.6%) of the 121 cases: 62 cases in the study group and 59 in the comparison group.

In examining the results of the referral to children's social care for the two groups it must be recalled that a greater proportion of cases in the study group (children living with a parent with learning disabilities) had been categorised as multiple problem cases. It would be expected that the difficulties faced by these families would be reflected in the service provision during the two-year follow-up period.

Re-referrals

Cases in the study group showed a similar pattern in relation to the rate of re-referrals to those in the comparison group. Thirty-eight per cent of cases in the study group were re-referred during the follow-up period compared with 44.8 per cent of those in the comparison group.

Service provided

The UK Government acknowledges the need for long-term support and services for people with learning disabilities (including those who are parents).

> Many people with learning disabilities need additional support and services throughout their lives. This means that they have a longer and more intensive involvement in public services than the vast majority of citizens. (Cope 2003)

The follow-up data show that cases in the study group were significantly more likely to continue to receive social work services (see Table A.8,

Appendix II). Practically two-thirds of cases in the study group remained open to children's social care compared with 22 per cent in the comparison group.

Moreover, parents in the study group were more likely to receive services in their own right (see Table A.9, Appendix II). At the point of follow-up the records suggest two-thirds (67.3%) of parents in the study group were receiving a service to meet their own needs, compared with 40.7 per cent of parents in the comparison group. However, these data should be treated with caution because children's social care had difficulty providing information on services other than those provided by social services or family centres. For example, information on attendance at services for substance misuse or anger management was not readily available.

Child Protection Register

Children in the study group were more likely to have had their names placed on the Child Protection Register during the two-year follow-up period (see Table A.10, Appendix II). One-quarter of children in the study group were registered compared with only 3.4 per cent of children in the comparison group.

Children looked after

Children in the study group were also more likely to have been looked after. One-fifth (22.6%, n=14) of children in the study group had been looked after for some period during the two-year follow-up, compared with only three children (5.1%) in the comparison group. Moreover, children in the study group tended to remain looked after for longer. All 14 children in the study group were looked after at the point of follow-up compared with only one child in the comparison group.

Care orders

Although very few care orders were made, children in the study group were more likely to be placed on care orders. Care orders were made in respect of seven children in the study group and one child in the comparison group; all the children were placed with foster carers.

Summary

- Parents with learning disabilities rarely approached children's social care for help. Practitioners generally made referrals on behalf of parents.

- Children living with parents with learning disabilities were more likely to be referred because of 'child protection concerns', 'other parenting issues', and 'parental learning disability'.

- Nearly every referral (89.5%) involving parents with learning disabilities resulted in some form of assessment (either an initial or a core assessment).

- The initial assessment identified that a greater proportion of the children living with parents with learning disabilities had developmental needs in every development dimension, difficulties in each of the parenting capacity dimensions, and problems in relation to every family and environmental factor.

- From the information found on the Initial Assessment Record the research team classified approximately one-third of the study group as experiencing multiple problems. Multiple problem cases were defined as those where severe problems were present in all three domains. This was a significantly greater proportion than was found in the comparison group or in earlier research on a large cross sample of referrals to ten local authorities carried out by the author (Cleaver *et al.* 2004). However, it is important not to pathologise all children who live with a parent with learning disabilities; two-thirds of cases where an initial assessment was carried out were *not* classified as having multiple problems.

- When an initial assessment was carried out on a child living with a parent with learning disabilities, the case was more likely to progress to a core assessment. As a greater proportion of children in this group were experiencing severe needs in all three domains, these decisions would appear entirely appropriate.

- There is some evidence to suggest social workers experienced greater difficulty in completing core assessments on time when a parent had learning disabilities.

- The Core Assessment Records identified (a) a larger proportion of children living with parents with learning disabilities had developmental needs, (b) a greater proportion of parents with learning disabilities were experiencing difficulties in meeting the needs of their children, and (c) more difficulties in relation to family and environmental factors.

- The Core Assessment Records showed that a high proportion of parents with learning disabilities (95.7%) also experienced issues that negatively impact on parenting, such as mental illness or substance misuse.

- The recorded information on services provided during a two-year follow-up was limited. What was available suggests that when children live with parents with learning disabilities:

  ◦ cases are more likely to remain open to children's social care

  ◦ a greater proportion of children become looked after

  ◦ children are more likely to have their name placed on the child protection register

  ◦ more parents receive services from adult social services or family centres.

- The extent of the difficulties identified by the initial and core assessment suggests the services provided are not adequately meeting the needs of children and families where adults have learning disabilities. Short-term interventions cannot address the changing levels of understanding and skills parents with learning disabilities need to acquire in order to parent their children as they grow up. These families will need continuing support until children reach adulthood. No single agency can meet their complex needs and a joint approach that involves statutory and voluntary agencies and draws on the strengths within the extended family and community may prove the most expedient.

Chapter 3

Involving Families in the Assessment Process

This chapter is based on the findings from the interviews with parents and social workers. The names of all the children and families have been changed to ensure the anonymity of those involved in the study. The sample consists of 23 cases where children were living with a parent with learning disabilities (the study group), and 42 cases where children were living with parent(s) who did not have a learning disability (the comparison group). The comparison group was made up of families interviewed as part of a previous study undertaken by the author (Cleaver *et al.* 2004). Families included in the study group were approached initially by their social worker; more details can be found in Appendix I. In the study group 14 interviews were carried out with a lone mother with learning disabilities, 6 with a lone father with learning disabilities, and 3 with both parents where one or both had learning disabilities. In the comparison group interviews were conducted with 39 lone mothers or female carers, 1 lone stepfather, and 2 with both parents.

The characteristics of the families

The families included in the interview study were identified from the larger case file sample and as a result the profile of the interview group broadly reflects that of the wider sample.

The children

The study group included more boys (n=14, 60.9%) than girls (n=9, 39.1%). In contrast the comparison group was slightly biased towards girls and included 23 girls (54.8%) and 19 boys (45.2%). The study group also included a greater proportion of young children. Half the children living with a parent with learning disabilities were aged five years or less compared with 38 per cent of children in the comparison group. This skew towards younger children reflects the findings from the case file study discussed in Chapter 2. Finally, a significant proportion of children in the study group had been registered as learning disabled. This applied to just over one-third (n=8) of the 23 children in the study group but to none of the children in the comparison group.

Parental learning disability

From the description of parents recorded in the social work case notes and the reports given by professionals in their interviews, it is clear that parents included in the study group fell within the definition of learning disability given in *Valuing People* (Cm 5086 2001, p.14, paragraph 1.5). The information about the parents' learning disability gave a clear indication of a significantly reduced ability from childhood to understand new or complex information and a reduced ability to cope independently. An individual's cognitive ability had frequently been assessed by the administration of standardised intelligence tests such as the Stanford–Binet (Terman and Merrill 1960) or the Wechsler Adult Intelligence Scale (Wechsler 1974). Test scores are generally interpreted in the following way. An IQ score of 70 or below suggests impaired cognitive ability, with mild learning disability being defined as a score between 70 and 55, moderate disability between 54 and 40, and severe disability below 40.

The information recorded on the Core Assessment Record about Ms Smith demonstrates evidence of the use of standardised intelligence tests.

> This gave verbal and performance IQ scores (on the Wechsler Adult Intelligence Scale) of between 50 and 69, indicating that she is in the lower half of the range associated with mild disability. On this result Ms Smith was seen as eligible to receive support from the Specialist Learning Disability Team from Adult Services.

The coexistence of more than one issue affecting parenting capacity

Many parents with learning disabilities were also experiencing a number of additional problems such as poor mental or physical health, substance misuse and/or domestic violence. Families frequently lived in poor housing, cut off from their extended family, community resources and friends. Meeting the needs of parents with learning disabilities who are experiencing additional difficulties is problematic because the skills to work with people with dual diagnosis are scarce and protocols for working with other agencies are often absent (Cope 2003).

Parenting children with learning disabilities

Children of parents with learning disabilities are at risk from inherited disabilities and developmental delay as a result of cultural factors (McGaw 2000). As noted earlier, eight of the study children had learning difficulties and practically half (n=11, 47.8%) the families in this study included at least one child with learning difficulties. In three families more than one child had learning difficulties (in one family two children and in two families three siblings had learning difficulties respectively).

Parenting children with learning difficulties is a demanding task because they may require, for example, special diets or close supervision. These additional needs place greater demands on any parent and may place children at greater risk of neglect unless parenting competencies are well developed (McGaw 2000; McGaw and Sturmey 1993). These findings suggest that many parents with learning disabilities have the extra challenge of caring for children with learning difficulties.

Parental understanding of why the family was in contact with children's social care

When parents and practitioners hold a similar understanding of why the family is in contact with children's social care, parents are more likely to co-operate and work with practitioners (Cleaver and Freeman 1995). In the majority of cases parents with learning disabilities held a similar view to social workers about why the family was in contact with children's social care. Almost three-quarters (73.9%) of parents broadly agreed with the social workers' report of why the family had been referred for assessment.

The following examples serve to illustrate shared perspectives on the reason for the referral drawn from the group of parents with learning disabilities. The first introduces Lynn aged five years who lives with her baby brother and their mother, who has learning disabilities.

Lynn's failure to thrive – medical appointments not being kept. Not attending school, not accessing treatment – speech therapy. Also the house was absolutely filthy, they had two or three dogs, and dog faeces were all over the house, in every room. There was rotting food in most rooms and bin bags full of rubbish which was very smelly. The conditions were amongst the worst I had ever seen. We had to get specialist help in to clean the house. Our own service would not do it. (Social worker)

The mother agreed with the social worker about the reason for the assessment.

Because we were not coping and things were getting very bad, the house was very dirty. It was smelling and the dogs were dirtying it. We were not coping. (Mother)

In a rather different scenario a similar shared understanding prevailed.

Three of the four children in this family are severely disabled and the older child [James aged 10 years] is acting as carer. Mother has learning disabilities. There has been a long history of domestic violence and mum has been assaulted by dad. There is also a history of dad's misuse of alcohol, which is associated with the domestic violence. (Social worker's reason for the assessment)

The mother understood the social worker's concerns.

I think it was because of my partner's violence and him hitting me and I thought that they thought the children were at risk. But I can't really remember much more. I think my learning disability was a problem. (Mother)

Explaining the purpose and process of the assessment

In order to understand the child's developmental needs and find out what is happening within the family, assessments should, whenever possible, be carried out in partnership with the child and his or her family, and in conjunction with colleagues in other relevant agencies. In planning an assessment, practitioners need to ensure that families understand why the assessment is taking place, what it will entail, and the timescale. Parents with learning disabilities value practitioners who show them respect and use simple and clear terms when communicating important issues (Morris 2004).

Social workers were very committed to the principle of working in partnership with parents and in every case where parents had a learning disability spent considerable time trying to explain clearly the purpose and process of the assessment. For example, in 78.9 per cent of cases involving parents with learning disabilities, social workers spent an hour or more during the first visit talking to parents about the assessment and what would happen. However, taking that amount of time to explain the assessment process was not unusual. In 64.9 per cent of cases in the comparison group a similar amount of time was spent explaining the assessment process to families where parents did not have a learning disability.

What differentiated the study group from the comparison group were the difficulties social workers experienced in enabling parents with learning disabilities to understand why they were being assessed and what the assessment would involve. At subsequent visits social workers needed to reinforce continually what had been said because they were unsure parents with learning disabilities remembered or had fully understood the first time. As a result social workers not only spent considerable time explaining the assessment during the initial visit, but took time to reiterate the messages at subsequent meetings in an effort to ensure parents understood what was going on and why.

The following quotation demonstrates the efforts social workers took to explain the reason and process of assessment to parents with learning disabilities.

> Mum's learning disability made it more difficult. I talked to her and carefully explained things in simple terms.

In some cases social workers depended on the help of family members to ensure that parents with learning disabilities understood. For example, in the following case of baby Carl (introduced in Chapter 2, p.25) the referral was made because:

> There were concerns about Sue's parenting skills and how she would cope with Carl. She has quite a severe learning disability and had been involved with a learning disability team for some time.

The social worker went on to explain how she made use of the maternal grandparent to help explain things to the parents, Jim and Sue.

> I did a careful verbal explanation, they were very wary of why we were going in. I think they understood what we were saying. Maternal grandma lived next door and she helped.

> I had about three sessions with her [Sue] and her partner. It was difficult to assess the full extent of their abilities and to what extent they were understanding what I was telling them. I left a copy of the assessment documents and I asked her mother to try and help her understand them. I then went

back and went through the dimensions with her and I used analogies. I tried to use her own childhood experiences.

Involving a close relative or friend can be helpful. The presence of a known and trusted person may give the parent with learning disabilities greater confidence to express his or her views or to ask questions. But there are also potential drawbacks. The person without a learning disability may dominate the interview, or be over-protective of the parent with learning disabilities, or exclude the parent from the conversation (Booth and Booth 1996). In other cases the task of explaining the assessment process was shared with other professionals.

> I had a meeting with mum and dad and explained the process – mum engaged in this where previously she had not. The team leader chaired this meeting and the health visitor, SureStart and the nursery were involved.

In no case within this small qualitative sample did the social worker from children's services involve the help of a specialist communication worker or the learning disabilities team within adult services in explaining the reason or process of the assessment.

The level of parents' understanding

The parents' stories suggest that they were aware that social workers had talked to them about the assessment. Over two-thirds (69.6%) of parents with a learning disability and 78.6 per cent of parents in the comparison group reported that their social worker had discussed the assessment with them.

> She told us about it. She explained it.

> They explained things to me – the social worker did it.

> (The recollections of two mothers with learning disabilities)

However, the time and effort social workers took over this task did not always culminate in the results they had hoped for. Social workers' fears that not all parents understood or remembered what was said were realistic. In a number of cases parents with learning disabilities were uncertain or could not recall anyone talking to them about the assessment. For example, some parents reported that no one had talked to them about the assessment or, if they had, they could not remember what had been said.

> Someone did tell me [about the assessment] or give me something, but I can't remember what. (Parent with learning disabilities)

However, in every case the social worker had tried to get parents to understand what was happening. This is illustrated in the following case where the mother could not recall anyone explaining things to her. The adult learning disability team had referred the case because the father had recently died of cancer and there were concerns that the mother with learning disabilities would not be able to cope with her three daughters, all of whom had learning disabilities.

> It was quite difficult with mum because of her learning disability. I did not really know how much she understood. It was very difficult, probably impossible, to explain concepts to her – I really had to keep it very simple and repeat things. The eldest daughter was of considerable help as she was the most capable member of the family. (Social worker)

Once again this case highlights the need to involve those with specialist skills in communicating with people with learning disabilities. It is of interest that, although working with the mother, the adult learning disability team was not involved in helping the social worker in children's services to communicate with the mother during the assessment.

> I feel that a joint assessment between children and adult services should have been done but they [adult services] would not agree to this. (Social worker)

However, the social worker was successful in involving adult social services in the provision of some services.

Involving parents in the assessment process

The implementation of the Assessment Framework and the use of the assessment records has increased the involvement of parents in the assessment process (Cleaver *et al.* 2004). The involvement of parents with learning disabilities proved more challenging. Although most of the study parents understood and could recall simple aspects of the assessment process, more complex issues proved harder. For example, most (n=21, 91.3%) parents with learning disabilities knew that during the assessment social workers sought to learn about their family. In contrast only half (n=11, 47.8%) knew, or were able to recall, social workers talking to them about getting information from other professionals. In all but two cases social workers assured the researcher that they had gone to considerable lengths to explain and seek parental permission prior to consulting other professionals.

To involve parents with learning disabilities successfully in the assessment process was difficult and time-consuming and depended on the skills and patience of the practitioner. Social workers have to take account of the difficulties parents may have in reading written information, in remembering verbal information, and in keeping their attention focused on the task in hand. In 14 of the 23 cases (61%) included in the study group, social workers expressed considerable concern that the learning disability was an obstacle to parents' full involvement in the assessment process. To involve parents successfully in the assessment process took time and ingenuity.

> The pace of working with a learning disabled mum and going through the reasons for involvement and the process was very time consuming. Also during interviews it took a lot longer than normal to get answers to questions. I had to be more creative in the way I put the questions. Some areas I could make very little progress in and was not able to satisfactorily complete those areas. However, I do think that spending time was well worth it in the end. (Social worker)

In trying to keep parents' attention focused on the assessment and the needs of their child in very complex cases, where family life was chaotic and demanding, a strategy some social workers used was to carry out some interviews in the social work office, a method of working highlighted by practitioners during one of the research feedback sessions. However, such an approach would need to be part of an overall plan, because by not routinely observing the living conditions and the interactions between parents and children, the child's developmental needs and living conditions may not be fully understood.

Using specialist skills and assessment tools

Families where children live with a parent with learning disabilities account for only a small proportion of all referrals to children's social care. As a result social workers in the children and families' teams could not be expected to have the specialist skills and expertise needed to work with people with learning disabilities. Indeed, inspections of services for disabled adults found assessment of parenting skills were often undertaken by staff who did not have the necessary skills (Goodinge 2000).

There was little evidence from the case files or the interviews with social workers that tools designed to assist in identifying the strengths and weaknesses of families where parents have learning disabilities were used. Specialist toolkits and guidelines do exist such as those produced by McGaw et al. (1999). McGaw (2000) provides a helpful description and review of their validity and explains which work well with adults with learning disabilities.

Moreover, Mackinnon, Bailey and Pink (2004) have produced a video-based training resource to support staff working with people with learning disabilities. More recently, parents with learning disabilities within the national organisation CHANGE have produced a training pack aimed at professionals working with families like their own (CHANGE 2005).

Social workers were much more likely to take advantage of family centres to assess parenting, a few of which made good use of specialist materials such as those developed by the Daventry Family Centre (Hopkins 2002). There is evidence, however, that parents with learning disabilities do not always feel comfortable or benefit from attending parenting groups when they are in the minority. These parents may have difficulty keeping pace with group learning and other parents may reject or alienate them, thus reinforcing a feeling of inadequacy (McGaw and Sturmey 1994).

Involving adult learning disability teams in the assessments of children and families was rare, and the difficulties of collaborative work with adult services was a theme at every stage of assessment and planning – an issue highlighted in previous research (Cotson *et al.* 2001). Moreover, involving practitioners from learning disability teams in adult services in assessments of children and families has resource implications.

The following case introduces Jade, aged ten years, and illustrates the difficulties of generating collaborative work. The mother had sought help for the following reasons.

> Jade had been assaulted in the street by a man in the village. We went for help. They knew we has learning difficulties, over the years we have struggled. (Mother)

This was a case well known to children's social care.

> They previously had a lodger who had allegedly raped mum and assaulted the children. We were concerned about the parents' ability to protect the children. There had also been a recent incident when it was alleged that Jade, who is not yet 10 years old, had been sexually assaulted by a man who lives in the village. Mum and dad both have a learning disability and mum seems to have some other health problems. (Social worker)

The social worker wanted to involve adult services during the core assessment to help explain things to the mother, but this proved difficult.

> Their level of understanding was such that I never accepted the first answer they [the parents] gave but tried to cover the issues in a number of different ways, and all of this took a long time. I tried to get the Adult Learning Disability team involved but they were very reluctant. (Social worker)

Barriers to inter-agency collaborative work

Government inspections of services to support disabled adults in their parenting role identified tensions and conflicts between adult social services and children's services that hamper joint work (Goodinge 2000; Wates 2002). The difficulties of effective working across adult and children's services have also been identified in previous research (see for example Cotson *et al.* 2001; Tarleton *et al.* 2006; Weir 2003). Of particular relevance in this study were the different thresholds for intervention between adult and children's services and variations between the eligibility criteria for family support services.

Both interviews with individual social workers and comments received during the research feedback sessions suggest practitioners from children's social care frequently experience difficulty in engaging adult social services learning disability teams in their work because the adult services operate high thresholds. This finding echoes previous research that explored the experiences of disabled parents (Morris 2003).

Although social workers went to great lengths to involve parents in the assessment process, they thought this process would have been enhanced if they could have worked with colleagues from adult services. The following case, introduced on pp.51–52, where there were concerns about five-year-old Lynn's failure to thrive, the dogs and the filthy conditions, shows that although other child care agencies are frequently involved during the assessment process adult services rarely participate at this stage.

> I saw mum and her mum together and spoke to aunty alone. I spent time explaining things to mum and grandma helped. Mum tended to be quiet. Mum had a moderate learning disability and grandma suffered from depression and she had a learning disability, but was more able than mum. They were very scared of our involvement and mum's learning disability made things more difficult. I spent time reasoning with them and explaining things very carefully. It was time-consuming. (Social worker)

In carrying out the assessment a range of other agencies were consulted. For example, the school, educational psychologist, speech therapist, educational welfare officer and school nurse contributed to the assessment of Lynn's developmental needs. In assessing the environmental factors that were adversely affecting the family, housing was involved. However, the learning disabilities team within adult services did not contribute to the assessment. The plan for Lynn and her family was quite comprehensive but it was unclear what provision was made for long-term support.

The plan included cleaning up the home, we found alternative homes for the three dogs. We arranged family centre support which included parenting skills sessions. The child was given an after-school play group place twice weekly. We negotiated a Community Care grant and arranged the involvement of a local voluntary group who provided bed-clothes and clothing for the child. The child received speech therapy and an educational psychologist became involved. The benefits section became involved with advice and support on benefits.

Parental acquiescence may affect professional judgement

Acquiescence, or the tendency to respond affirmatively regardless of what is asked, may be an adaptive response by those brought up in institutions 'to the demands of living when the greater part of their lives is under someone else's control' (Booth and Booth 1996, p.37). Today it can be argued that parents with learning disabilities are less likely to have grown up in institutions and more likely to have experienced the challenges of day-to-day living within the community.

Nonetheless, informal discussions with academics working in this field suggest that the life experiences of adults with learning disabilities have left them feeling particularly powerless. When addressed by social workers or others whom they perceive as powerful (including university researchers), parents with learning disabilities tend to agree with everything said to them in an effort to please. It is difficult for social workers or other professionals to get behind this wish to please, and understand their true views, wishes and feelings. The following case illustrates not only the time and effort social workers spent in explaining things to parents but also how the eagerness of parents with learning disabilities to agree with professionals may influence social workers' judgements. It introduces Katie, aged four years, who was referred for the following reasons.

Allegations that dad had sexually abused Katie. The mum says she was sexually abused by her dad when she was a child. Katie's name not placed on the Child Protection Register. The health visitor raised some concerns about mum's ability to cope with Katie and their newborn baby. Mum is learning disabled, the case was referred to the learning disabled team but mum refused, otherwise they would have done an assessment. Her level of comprehension is difficult to establish. Dad also has a learning disability. (Social worker)

Once again joint working with adult learning disability teams was frustrated, but in this instance the mother's unwillingness to attend, rather than organisational issues, was the stumbling block. Working without the advantage of the expertise of the learning disabilities team, the social worker spent considerable time trying to involve the parents in the assessment process but remained uncertain how much was understood.

> I saw them individually and together. They like attention and were quite positive, mum especially. The main problem was knowing whether or not they understood what was happening and what I was saying to them. They said that they did, but I had doubts. They both tended to agree with things. (Social worker)

This tendency of parents with learning disabilities to agree with what was said was a recurring theme in the interviews with social workers and during feedback sessions and may influence social work practice. Social workers raised concerns that services to support families may be continued without objectively reviewing their impact on the children's development, because of the parents' willingness to co-operate. It is the very passivity and acquiescence to social work plans that feeds the optimism of professionals and, it could be argued, in some cases results in children being left in conditions that place them at risk of significant harm.

Parental experiences of assessments and plans

Not all assessments led to plans for the child and family. When plans had been made, parents with learning disabilities were less likely to be aware of them or consider them to be helpful. For example, although a Child in Need Plan existed in 22 of the 23 cases in the study group, only 15 parents (68.2%) were aware of the plans, and only 7 of these parents (46.7%) felt the plan would be of real benefit to their family. Parents in the comparison group were more aware of what was going on and expressed greater satisfaction. In 36 cases in this group where plans had been made, 30 (83.3%) parents knew of them and 24 (80%) of these parents thought the plan would definitely help their child and family.

The following is an example of a parent with learning disabilities who felt fully involved in the assessment process and considered that the plan had benefited her family. Mrs Barnes is learning disabled and suffers from depression. She has had seven children, none of whom she was able to care for on a full-time basis. Tom, her 14-year-old son, lived with his elder sister, but serious behavioural difficulties resulted in his returning to live with his mother. She explained the reason she had sought the help of children's social care.

> Tom and me were at loggerheads and I was depressed and I was getting panic attacks and the school seemed to get a bit concerned and told me I should talk to social services. Tom was also staying out all hours. (Mrs Barnes)

> I wanted and needed help and advice so Tom and me could get on better with each other. I just wanted help to get things right and I wanted help with being depressed. (Mrs Barnes)

When talking about what happened as a result of the plans Mrs Barnes explained:

> They have helped with Tom. They have taken him on day trips and they helped him to join the army cadets and he's doing well. We are getting on better now, a lot better.

In another case the mother, Mrs Jones, felt involved in the assessment process but had mixed feelings about the resulting plan. The social worker explains the reason for the referral:

> The school said that Steven [a boy aged 10 years] was coming into school very smelly, dirty and that he had lice. He was also having dental problems, and dental appointments were not being kept. The school was concerned that Steven was being neglected and this had been going on for some time. (Social worker)

Steven's mother held a similar understanding about why children's social care was in contact with her family.

> Everything went downhill. Steven was not getting the right care from me. Some days OK, other days downhill. I split up with his dad some years ago and then I separated from my new man a few months ago. And everything got bad. (Mrs Jones)

> I wanted them to help me get back on the right track. I just wanted help in looking after Steven. I was not caring for Steven properly and they said I was neglecting him. (Mrs Jones)

This mother's experience of the assessment was also positive. She felt the social worker had asked what help she wanted, she understood that the social worker would be collecting information about her family, and felt she had been consulted at all times.

> He always kept me informed about who he wanted to speak to and who he contacted about me. (Mrs Jones)

She knew what the plans were, but had mixed feelings about them.

> They said they'd help me in the home to get it cleaner and help me to keep it clean. They also said that Steven's name was to go on the register and it's still on… I was pleased they were going to help me in the home, but I didn't like the register. (Mrs Jones)

In the third case, involving Sandy, a newborn baby, the father was less certain about the assessment process and did not agree with the plan. The social worker's report explains why children's social care was in contact with the family.

> There has been a previous history of abuse by mum against her children who have been removed. Mum suffers from mental health problems, dad has a learning disability but functions reasonably well and he holds down a job, but he cannot read or write. He has, however, developed a strategy for budgeting. An advocate has been appointed to help him. Mum is now in residential care and it was thought that dad could not manage to parent a child. The child was placed with foster carers directly from hospital. A police protection order was taken, mum attempted to remove the child from the hospital. (Social worker)

> The core assessment identified that neither mum nor dad were able to care for the child, and it helped us to make the decision to go for a full care order and possibly adoption. (Social worker)

Sandy's father understood why the social worker was carrying out an assessment, but did not share her views of his parenting skills.

> They thought that I couldn't really look after the baby and it was difficult for me. They thought we couldn't look after the baby. They thought the baby wasn't safe with us and they wanted to see if we could manage and they thought we couldn't. (Sandy's father)

This father had considerable difficulty recalling what had happened during the assessment process. For example, although the social worker had taken considerable time explaining the reason and process of the assessment and sought his agreement before consulting other professionals, he could recall little or none of this. He could not remember whether the social worker had asked him what help he wanted or whether he minded if other professionals were approached for information. His dissatisfaction with the resulting plan, however, was clear.

> I didn't like them, I didn't want the baby taken away. I wanted to keep the baby but they wouldn't let me, they took him away and he's still away. (Sandy's father)

These illustrations involving parents with learning disabilities mirror the pattern found for other parents (Cleaver *et al.* 2004). Parental satisfaction with the outcome of assessments was related to:

- a shared perspective between parents and social workers on the difficulties families were facing
- involvement in the choice and development of the plans
- agreement with and commitment to the plan
- the plan coming to fruition.

The findings suggest that what differentiates parents with learning disabilities is the additional time social workers need to spend in communicating with parents using concrete concepts that they can understand. To involve parents with learning disabilities successfully in the assessment process may require additional skills and expertise and the use of specifically designed tools. It is a very time-consuming process because parents with learning disabilities may experience great difficulty in understanding abstract notions and complex issues. Appointing an advocate when cases come to court (as happened with Sandy's father) is one way of ensuring people with learning disabilities are not discriminated against (Cm 5086 2001).

Summary

- Parents with learning disabilities frequently experience a range of other issues that affect their parenting, such as poor physical and mental health, substance misuse and domestic violence.
- Practically half the families involved in the study also had the additional challenge of parenting at least one child with learning disabilities.
- Housing is frequently poor, and in many instances parents with learning disabilities have difficulty in keeping the home conditions hygienic. Social workers have suggested during feedback sessions that the decline in local authority accommodation has left parents with learning disabilities particularly disadvantaged. They must now negotiate with private landlords who may be less tolerant and understanding of people with learning disabilities than local authority housing departments.
- Social workers were committed to involving parents with learning disabilities in the assessment process and planning. Despite considerable time and effort spent in explaining things to parents

and reinforcing key messages at subsequent interviews, in many cases social workers remained uncertain how much was understood or retained.

- In some cases, in order to facilitate communication with parents with learning disabilities, social workers involved a relative or close friend.

- There was little collaborative work between adult and children's services. In the majority of cases adult services did not contribute to the assessment. In some cases social workers had tried to involve adult learning disabilities teams in the assessment process but experienced difficulties, because parents were not seen to reach the threshold for adult assessment or services. In other cases social workers did not seek the assistance of adult services, or parents refused to work with adult services.

- Parents with learning disabilities were generally passive and eager to agree with the suggestions and plans professionals put forward. This willingness had an impact on social workers' judgements in two ways: first, it was difficult for social workers to know the true views and wishes of parents; second, it encouraged professionals to think that parents understood plans for their child and family and were able to translate them into action.

Chapter 4

The Provision of Services
and Outcomes for Children

The previous two chapters compared the responses of children's social care to referrals of children living with parents with learning disabilities to a cross-section of all referrals. This chapter focuses solely on children living with parents with learning disabilities. The aim was to follow up all cases in the original sample of children living with a parent with learning disabilities three years after the referral. However, at the initial data-gathering stage in ten instances the case number had not been available and in a further two cases changes to the authority's recording system made identifying the cases impossible at the point of follow-up. As a result 12 cases were lost to the study. This chapter is based on the findings for 64 cases.

Children separated from parents with learning disabilities
Adopted children
Following up the cases revealed that two of the 64 children (3.1%) had been adopted as a result of the original contact with children's social care. One case involved an unborn child and the other a child aged between three and four years. A review of these two cases reveals that both had been referred because there were concerns over the child's safety and welfare. The child assessments suggest the decisions to free these two children for adoption had been evidence-based.

In the first example, we return to Sandy, the newborn baby (see p.62). The following information was taken from the case file and shows the circumstances that led children's social care to remove Sandy permanently from the care of his parents.

> Initial referral received informing the Department that Ann Moore was pregnant. Ms Moore had had extensive social work input in the past which has culminated in her four children being removed. They were made the subject of care orders and three placed in long-term foster placements and the other child being adopted in 1996. A prebirth assessment was attempted with Ms Moore and her new partner. Neither parent engaged and it was apparent that both parents would struggle to meet the needs of their newborn baby due to learning difficulties. The local authority convened an initial child protection conference and it was agreed that the baby's name be placed on the Child Protection Register at birth and legal proceedings initiated as soon as the baby was born.
>
> Ms Moore agreed for the local authority to accommodate him voluntarily on their discharge from hospital prior to legal proceedings commencing. However, on 27 July Ms Moore attempted to remove Sandy from the hospital. Police powers of protection were effected and Sandy was placed with foster carers. The local authority applied for an Emergency Protection Order (EPO) to secure Sandy's wellbeing which was granted. Legal proceeding commenced. Both partner and Ms Moore made separate representations as a carer for Sandy. Contact continued on a regular basis separately with both parents.
>
> At the beginning of a contact session Ms Moore became very aggressive and again tried to remove Sandy from the care of the local authority. She assaulted the social worker present and was informed that contact would be stopped for a seven-day period. The local authority applied for an order to cease contact between Sandy and Ms Moore. At the hearing Ms Moore again became very angry and left. The order was granted unopposed.
>
> Partner and Ms Moore's legal representative requested a full psychological assessment of each respondent. This was jointly funded by all parties. Partner and Ms Moore were assessed by Mr W., who concluded that neither parent either separately or jointly would be able to care for Sandy due to their low cognitive abilities and difficulty in understanding the abstract developmental needs of a growing child. The final hearing was delayed as partner requested a residential assessment be undertaken with Sandy. The local authority opposed this as it believed that it would not be in anyone's interest. However, at the hearing to consider the assessment, partner became distressed and he left the court. His application was disregarded. Sandy was made the subject of a care order and freed for adoption. Sandy was placed with his new adoptive family on [date removed]. The adoption order was granted. (Social worker's report)

The assessment of the other adopted child, a girl aged between three and four years, highlighted the difficulties the mother was experiencing. In addition to her learning disability she was physically disabled, had poor mental health, had a sensory impairment, a history of domestic violence and had herself been brought up in local authority care. The family fulfilled the research criteria for families experiencing multiple problems; that is, the child had severe developmental needs *and* the mother was experiencing severe difficulties in meeting her child's needs *and* there were severe difficulties in relation to family and environmental factors. Following the assessment a number of services had been provided, prior to the child being looked after and eventually freed for adoption, including help from adult services, the voluntary sector and a family centre.

The social work reports and other information held on the case files of both children who were adopted suggest the decisions were taken only after considerable service input from a range of different agencies had failed to ensure the children could remain living safely at home.

Looked-after children

Nine children were excluded from the follow-up study because they had been looked after for at least the last 12 months. In eight cases (six boys and two girls) children were fostered with non-relatives and in one case with maternal grandparents. Five of the eight children fostered with non-relatives were on care orders and all the other children were accommodated under s20 of the Children Act 1989. The group included children of all ages: two children were aged between 0 and 2 years, another two between 3 and 4 years, two children were aged between 5 and 9 years, and four young people were between the ages of 10 and 14 years at the time of referral.

In most cases (n=7) the children had been referred because of child protection concerns; one case was referred because of the parent's learning disability. In two cases, referred by adult services because of concerns about the parents' capacity to safeguard their children, no social work assessment was found on the case file. The referral resulted directly in enquiries being carried out under s47 and a care order being granted.

The social worker's assessment and the enquiries suggested all the families were experiencing serious difficulties, and revealed the many problems affecting parenting capacity. For example, in addition to a learning disability in three cases the parents had poor mental health, in three cases a physical disability, in five cases a sensory impairment, in three cases parents had themselves experienced childhood abuse, five children were exposed to domestic violence, and in two cases parents had a history of abusing children. In addition three children themselves had learning disabilities. Finally, five cases fulfilled the research criteria for families experiencing multiple problems. Once again the assessments suggest that social workers' decisions to place children away from home were not taken precipitately.

The social work files indicated that once placed with foster carers all the children showed progress, as the following cases illustrate.

> Charles was described as absolutely fabulous in his foster placement. His level of understanding of the world has dramatically improved. His improvements have been so consistent that he is now ready to move on to a long-term placement. (Social worker's report on Charles who has learning difficulties, aged 5–9 years)

> Kyle is doing well in his placement, meeting his targets and developing well. His personality is really coming out and he is showing many different emotions which is seen as positive. His foster carer is given respite one night every two weeks. (Social worker's report on Kyle who has learning difficulties, aged 3–4 years)

> Jenny experienced emotional, physical and sexual abuse whilst in the care of her parents. She has made significant progress whilst being in foster care. She attends school for children with mild learning difficulties and has a statement of SEN. (Social worker's notes on Jenny who has learning difficulties, aged 10–14 years)

Besides the nine children fostered for over 12 months, a further child, Katie (see p.59), became looked after more recently.

> Referral made by mum. Mum called the emergency duty team to ask if they could arrange for her six-year-old daughter to be taken into care. Mum was crying and said she could not cope. Katie is apparently hitting people, punching them, kicking walls and furniture. Mum has also caught Katie touching her younger sister down below. Mum is staying with a friend tonight for support. Mum said that parents from school had been ringing up saying that Katie wants to kiss all the lads, etc. I asked if Katie had experienced any sexual behaviour/abuse from others and mum said no, but when I checked ISSIS [electronic recording system] it is clear that this is not the case and she has experienced sexual abuse from her step father. Mum has been in hospital with kidney trouble and the stress of dealing with Katie. She also feels depressed and that she can't cope anymore. Katie was accommodated under s20 – volutary accommodation. (Social worker's notes on Katie aged six years at the time she was accommodated)

The illustrations show that in no case had a child been removed from the care of his or her parents solely because the parent had a learning disability. Parental learning disability was compounded by other issues such as poor parental mental and physical health, domestic violence, substance misuse, isolation from family and friends, poverty and inadequate housing, and in every case there were substantiated concerns for the child's safety and welfare.

The profile of children living with parents with learning disabilities

Three years after the referral 52 children (81.3%) were continuing to live with parents with learning disabilities.

Members of the household

In two-thirds of cases (n=35, 67.3%) all the adults in the household had a learning disability. For example, at the point of follow-up (at least three years after the child was referred) 18 children lived with their mother and father, both of whom had a learning disability, and one child moved between his mother's and his father's household (again both had learning disabilities). A further 16 children lived in a household where the mother with a learning disability was the only adult. Thus, practically one-third of mothers with a learning disability (30.8%) were bringing up their children without the support of another adult.

The following report on the parents' learning disability relates to a family of eight children.

> Both parents learning disabled. Mother is sociable but impressionable and eager to please. She can manage some domestic tasks but has limited understanding of money. She has a poor short-term memory. Father was slow to talk as a child. He is good with his hands, practical and not academic. He suffers from deafness in his right ear. Father also has a history of mental illness. (Social worker's report)

In one-third of cases (n=17, 32.7%) an adult who did not have a learning disability was involved in the day-to-day care of the child. For example, nine children lived with their mother (with learning disabilities) and their father or mother's partner who did not have a learning disability. In the other eight cases the care of the children was shared with relatives or professionals. Three children lived with a parent and another adult relative, such as mother's sister or father's parents, one child lived at home but in a shared care arrangement with non-related foster carers, and four children lived with their mother in a refuge for victims of domestic violence.

The challenge of parenting for parents with learning disabilities was compounded because they were frequently caring for more than one child – a situation found in over three-quarters of cases (82.6%). For example, in 20 cases the study child was living at home with two siblings, in 6 cases with three siblings and in 17 cases with four or more siblings.

Age and gender of the children

The ages of children who continued to live with their parents reflected the study group referred to children's social care. For example, half the children (50%) were below the age of five years, less than one-third (26.9%) were aged between five and nine years, and young people aged ten years or more accounted for approximately one-fifth (23%) of the group.

The original sample contained a slightly larger proportion of boys than girls and this trend became stronger in the group of children who continued to live with their parents. The group was made up of 32 boys (61.5%) and 20 girls (38.5%).

Children with disabilities

The follow-up scrutiny of the social work case files provided in-depth information about the types of disabilities and health issues children were experiencing and suggests that the earlier data underestimated the situation. The findings show that 29 of the 52 children had one or more forms of disability. For example, 23 children had learning disabilities (18 of whom had a statement of education needs), 5 children had a hearing disability, 7 had impaired vision, in 18 cases the child's ability to communicate was impaired, and 3 children were incontinent. Children were also plagued by chronic health problems. Eight children were asthmatic, two suffered from epilepsy, one had a spinal injury, and one had severe bowel problems. The following social worker's report on Larry, aged eight years, illustrates the chronic health issues some children are experiencing.

> Larry has an artificial right limb as this leg is significantly shorter. Larry has speech and language difficulties as well as a significant learning disability and he suffers from cardiac problems. Larry receives more care from his father to do with his physical disability. His father helps him in and out of the bath and when he needs to go upstairs to go to the toilet then he has to

take his prosthetic leg off. The school has contacted the physiotherapist as Larry's leg appears to be too short again.

Caring for a child with disabilities is a challenge for any parent – a circumstance acknowledged by the government in their definition of a child in need (s17, 10(c)). For parents with learning disabilities the challenges are far greater and accessing help more difficult. The propensity for adults with learning disabilities to comply with professionals (discussed earlier) is likely to influence their capacity to champion their children and negotiate with a variety of different agencies and professionals to ensure their children receive the most appropriate and timely services (an issue that frequently daunts articulate parents). Unless families receive on-going support and specialist help it is unlikely that these children will have their needs adequately met, let alone reach their full potential.

Legal status of the children

In the majority of cases (n=46, 88.5%) at the point of follow-up statutory orders did not apply to children who were living with their parents. The findings show that care orders applied to two siblings who lived with their parents, a residence order was in place for one child who lived with her mother and her mother's sister, and orders prohibiting contact with their father were in place for two children in another family.

The names of 23 children had, during the follow-up period, been placed on the child protection register. Most registrations (n=20) related to children who did not become looked after or adopted. Although the names of more than one-third of children (38.5%) who had continued to live with their parents had at some point been placed on the register, all but two had been removed at the point of follow-up. Children had been registered for a variety of reasons. In 11 cases the reason for registration was neglect, in 8 cases physical abuse, in 1 case emotional and sexual abuse, and in 3 cases the reason had not been recorded on the case file. The following serve as illustrations.

> All of the children's names were placed on the child protection register under category of physical abuse, after Jamie [aged 7 years] made allegations of being punched by his father.

> All three children's names placed on CPR due to Mum's failure to engage with agencies and the neglect of her children.

> Unborn baby registered because mother was living with a schedule 1 offender – he moved away.

Significant changes to the household

Instability and change is a feature in the lives of many children in contact with children's social care (Ward, Munroe and Dearden 2006). The children of parents with a learning disability are no different. For example, in 19 cases (36.5%) the child moved house at least once during the three-year follow-up period. The case files suggest families moved for a variety of reasons. Some were positive, such as the result of re-housing, while others were more negative, for example as a result of harassment by neighbours or child abuse.

> The last neighbourhood was very difficult – the cul-de-sac was 'clicky'. The neighbour had mental health problems. When things deteriorated the parents were not able to defend themselves and dad began to spend a lot of time away from home. Hence the unhygienic conditions of the children. The children experienced verbal abuse from the neighbours, giving rise to frightening behaviour by George and Jamie. (Social worker's notes on George and Jamie)

> Family moved from living next door to paternal grandfather after allegations of abuse of Jade by paternal grandfather. (Social worker's notes on Jade who has learning difficulties, aged 10 years, see p.57)

Not only did many children and parents undergo geographic changes but practically half (n=23, 44.2%) experienced changes to the composition of their household. Many children were separated from their fathers. In five cases the mother left the child's father, taking her children with her, and in six cases the child's father or male carer (mother's partner) moved out; one father returned to live with his family. The father of one child died.

Other children experienced separation from their mothers. One child was removed from his mother by his father to live with his own parents. Two mothers (one the mother of seven children and the other the mother of only one child) left their children in the fathers' care; both mothers returned after a short period.

The following introduces Sam aged 18 months. It is a case where the mother left the home for a short period but was able finally to be reunited.

> Mum briefly moved out of the home to live with her sister-in-law because of the injuries to Sam (bruises to both cheeks, scratch/bruising to the left shoulder and scratches on cheeks, three fading marks on left leg on thigh muscle, these marks were similar in outline to finger marks). It is thought that mum caused these injuries.

This information was gathered from a review 12 months later:

> Mum visits with dad as supervisor of contact. It is felt this should continue and increase. There is no doubt in mum and dad's minds that failure to protect the children would see the Directorate removing them. However, the love and caring between all members of this family shows a level of commitment which can be worked with and hopefully be successful in reuniting the family as a unit. (Social worker's report on Sam; both parents have learning disabilities as does Sam and his sister)

The case notes show that Sam's mother did indeed return to the family home.

A few children were separated from other significant relatives such as siblings and grandparents. For example, the older sibling of one child moved away. In another case the mother and her child moved from the grandparents home to live independently. The grandmother of a further child died.

Services provided to meet children's needs

Once again there is attrition in the data set and information was available on only 45 cases. At the initial stage of the study no assessment identifying children's needs was found on the case file for seven children who continued to live with their parents. As a result it has not been possible to include these cases in the examination of whether services were provided to meet identified needs.

Additional problems arose because of recording practice and the local authority's system to support recording. The idiosyncratic recording styles meant the research team experienced considerable difficulty locating information about service provision within the case files (whether paper or computer based). For example, in relation to services provided to meet the child's developmental needs no information could be discerned in 13 cases, to support parenting capacity no information was found in 15 cases, and to address family and environmental difficulties no information was found in 12 cases.

Services to support children's developmental needs

Where information about service provision had been recorded this suggests that in practically every case where the child's developmental needs were identified planned services had been provided. For example, in 20 cases children had health needs and in every case where information was available on the social work record, it indicated a service was provided.

HEALTH NEEDS

Jade, aged 10 years (see p.57 and p.72), lives with her mother who has learning disabilities and her two siblings both with learning dificulties. The original concerns of sexual abuse arose when Jade was six years old: a referral from the health visitor identified the following: 'query re. Jade being sexually abused by a couple of boys'. The next referral came three years later from the Police Child Protection Unit: 'Jade had been sexually assaulted by an adult male in the village.' This resulted in the adult male being charged and found guilty of offences against Jade. The most recent allegation was that Jade was being sexually abused by her grandfather who lived next door. Although Jade had experienced a history of sexual abuse the intervention focused on more practical issues.

> *Identified issue.* Jade's hygiene continues to be poor and in the home bath nights are Tuesdays, Thursdays and Sundays, but Jade will not co-operate.

> *Planned services.* The school nurse will do some work on hygiene and puberty and Jade will be involved in this.

EDUCATIONAL NEEDS

A similar service response was found in relation to children's needs in other aspects of their development. For example, attempts were made to encourage regular school attendance as illustrated by the case of Lynn, aged eight years (see pp.51–52 and p.58).

> *Identified issue.* [The social worker's record notes] at the time of the referral concerns expressed at lack of attendance at school and poor time-keeping, signs of neglect, dirty clothes, hungry and smelling of body odour. [The assessment noted] Lynn's speech is a matter of concern and she will soon have an assessment completed by a speech therapist.

> *Service provided.* [The social worker's case closure report shows the results of the intervention] Lynn now attends school regularly, speech therapy programme completed with success, 1–1 sessions still ongoing in school, family have kept all appointments and attend family group meetings. Both Surestart and Homestart involved with family.

Lynn lives with her learning-disabled mother at her grandmother's home; her aunt also lives there.

Services were also provided to meet childen's needs in relation to other developmental dimensions as the following examples illustrate.

EMOTIONAL AND BEHAVIOURAL DEVELOPMENT

Fred, aged three years, has some degree of learning difficulties and lives with his mother who has a learning disability. Following the assessment the Child in Need Plan identified a number of agencies who agreed to work with the child and family.

> *Identified issue.* Has temper outbursts and temper tantrums. Mum stated that he seems to attack visitors when they visit their home.

> *Planned services.* Social services, NCH, support with behaviour management and coping techniques. It was identified in the family social work supervision that Families First was a possible support for Fred's mother to continue her parenting of Fred. This was discussed with Fred's mother who was willing to try anything. A referral was made to Families First.

IDENTITY

Paul's case provides an example of parents who were experiencing difficulties in helping their child develop a sense of identity. Paul is seven years old and lives with his mother who has learning disabilities and suffers from depression. Also living at home are Paul's two sisters and his brother. His stepfather who lives with the family has an alcohol problem.

> *Identified issue.* Parents do not appear to understand the importance of recognising the individuality of their children nor the extra effort they should be making due to Mother's special needs, lack of birth father, poor relationship with step dad and the arrival of a new baby girl.

> *Planned services.* Paul to attend the after school club.

FAMILY AND SOCIAL RELATIONSHIPS

Robbie, aged nine years, provides an example of how difficulties in children's family and social relationships were addressed. Robbie has severe autism which affects his relationship with his siblings, and is particularly upsetting to his six-year-old sister, Lucy. His mother explained the difficulties.

> Robbie can't let us know much. He makes noises and keeps on clapping his hands which annoys the other kids, especially Lucy, who gets wound up with him. Robbie wants a lot of care. We spend a lot of time on him.

The Child in Need Plan identified the following under the catergory of family and social relationships.

Identified issue. There is some sibling rivalry between Robbie and his siblings which can cause arguments due to there being no boundaries with the children.

Services provided. 15 hours per week from family support worker plus additional hours if needed. Reduced to 10 hours as things improved.

The report from the family support worker showed that the intervention had been successful: 'Rivalry has decreased. Parents now working together.' The respite was much appreciated by Robbie's parents, as his mother explained:

> It is a help that he goes to respite, but then I miss him and I want to cry, but I have to let him go to respite. We could not cope without it.

In only two cases were developmental needs identified and no appropriate services planned. These related to needs in emotional and behavioural development and family and social relationships for two children.

The assessment of children's developmental needs generally resulted in specific issues being identified. As a result plans were targeted at addressing the identified problem. When this had been resolved or there was evidence of improvement the case was generally closed to children's social care. However, this approach to planning does not allow for future difficulties to be anticipated and contingency plans to be developed.

Unfortunately, although the children's plans detailed the recommended services, the social work records did not always note whether services were forthcoming or whether families took advantage of the services offered to them.

Services to support parenting capacity

Where information was available, a similar pattern of planned service provision was found to support parents in meeting their children's needs for basic care, safety, emotional warmth, stimulation, guidance and boundaries, and stability. For example, the social work record indicates that in all but one case, some services were planned to address shortcomings in basic care and safety and, except for two cases, families received help in supporting them to provide emotional warmth, stimulation, guidance and boundaries, and stability. The following are examples of the types of services planned and/or provided to parents to support them in addressing their children's needs.

BASIC CARE

Greg is 11 years old and has learning difficulties and hearing and communication difficulties. He lives with his two siblings and their mother who has learning disabilities. The assessment identified that his mother was experiencing difficulties in meeting his basic needs and those of his siblings.

Identified issue. Greg was not always cleaned after soiling himself, all three children were losing weight and there was often no food in the house.

Services provided. To support the mother, children's social care and Family Care visited twice a week to help her establish routines.

The review shows the services that were provided and their impact.

Family Care have assisted mum in establishing routines concerning the children's bathing and laundry of clothes. Mum is working well and cooperating with Family Care and other agencies to improve the standard of her care of the children. She takes on board constructive criticism and advice. I have noticed, however, that the former depends on how the comments have been phrased as she can sometimes become defensive if she feels people are getting at her. A program of parenting assessment to look at mum's ability to retain information was drawn up. However, for a variety of reasons mum was unable to attend these planned meetings and as a consequence most had to be cancelled. Some work has been done with mum, including work on a genogram, a personal profile of parental perceptions, budgeting, routines, shopping, healthy diet, hygiene and home observations.

ENSURING SAFETY

Two-year-old Patrick lives with his mother in a refuge for women experiencing domestic violence. His mother, who has a learning disability, moved to the refuge because of the violence she was experiencing from Patrick's father. Patrick's mother has had her four other children taken into care. The social work record notes that Patrick's mother is having difficulties meeting Patrick's needs.

Identified issue. Patrick has recently been in hospital as Sally [Mother] felt he had a fever. However, the staff in the refuge felt concerned as Sally had been giving Patrick too much medication and they felt his welfare was at risk. Sally does struggle with times and does not prepare meals for Patrick. Sally does not have a routine for Patrick and her concept of Patrick's needs is poor. The staff at the refuge are concerned about what Sally is feeding Patrick, they say he has fish fingers for breakfast. Sally uses a pack of 24 nappies in one day and does not have any concept of money.

Services provided. Due to the concern reported by the refuge staff social services agreed to look after the child under s.20 of the 1989 Act – voluntary care. Cornerstones [a project offering support to vulnerable families] to support mother.

STIMULATION

Dan, aged eight months, lives with his parents, both of whom have learning disabilities, and his two half-siblings.

Identified issue and services provided. Parents have received advice and guidance in respect of stimulation from both health visitors and the family centre. Their ability to demonstrate and continue to offer appropriate stimulation is questionable.

GUIDANCE AND BOUNDARIES

Jean, aged 16 years, lives with her mother who has a learning disability and her stepfather. She has three siblings, including her severely autistic brother, Robbie.

Identified issue. [Social worker noted that] Mum finds it difficult to assert her authority.

Services provided. Written contract on the file between Jean and her parents about life at home, signed by all parties.

The findings in respect of the provision of services to address shortcomings in parenting capacity show the same patterns as those found in relation to addressing children's developmental needs. Services tended to be time-limited and provided to address specific issues or to ensure the mother learnt a particular task. Once this had been accomplished the likelihood was for the service to be discontinued and the case closed. The next crisis would trigger a further flurry of activity and agency interventions.

Services to support family and environmental factors

When examining how well difficulties relating to the wider family and environment were addressed the follow-up data suggest that in the majority of cases some efforts were made to address the difficulties, as the following cases illustrate.

FAMILY HISTORY AND FUNCTIONING

Dick, aged three years, lives with his baby sister and their mother and father. The mother has learning disabilities and the father, who is the main carer, experiences bouts of manic depression.

> *Identified issue.* [The social worker noted that] although mum goes to her parents' home when dad is ill, both mum and dad want to be as independent of them as they possibly can.

> *Planned services.* [The initial child protection plan addressed the issues in the following way:] Maternal gran to be approached to provide a structured plan of support via a written agreement. Adult mental health team to be approached in respect of assessing dad's home circumstances and the opportunity of offering help for the family with issues of home practicalities. Contingency plan to be considered by core group in respect of dad's illness to include respite foster care for both children to allow dad to recuperate.

SOCIAL RESOURCES

Susan, aged eight years, who has learning disabilities, lives with her brother and their parents (both of whom have mild learning disabilities).

> *Identified issue.* [The social worker noted] Susan and Scott appear to be isolated when not at school as peers are not encouraged to visit the home. Neither child belongs to any commmunity groups... Susan and Scott socialise at school only.

> *Services provided.* Suggestions of going to the park in warmer weather or to feed the ducks have been met with a further lack of understanding of why this should be bothered with. (Social worker's report)

HOUSING

Terry, aged five years, has physical and learning disabilities. He lives with his younger sister and their parents, both of whom have learning disabilities.

> *Identified issue.* The house requires alterations to provide wheelchair access etc. for Terry.

> *Services provided.* I am pleased to inform you that the provision of adaptations to the house has been provisionally approved and the OT13 referral form passed to architectural services for financial and technical checks to be made. Subject to these checks proving satisfactory the work will be carried out asap. (Social worker's report)

However, in a few cases although the assessment identified issues in relation to family and environmental factors, the recorded plan did not appear to

address them. The following case serves as an example. The assessment identified the following concerns.

> Housing conditions are currently poor and the family are vulnerable to
> eviction. Mum is currently staying with a friend who is supportive but has
> been asked to leave.

There was no record of any planned action or services being provided to
address the housing issue.

Administrative outcomes for children

Administrative outcomes were available for 52 cases. An exploration of the
group of children who continued to live with their parents showed that
the majority of cases (n=41, 78.8%) were closed to children's social care after
the first assessment and subsequent intervention.

The social workers' closure record suggests that cases were closed because
social workers judged parenting had improved sufficiently to ensure children's welfare and safety could be maintained while living at home through
the provision of universal services and/or specialist services other than
children's social care. However, of the 41 closed cases 23 were re-referred to
children's social care within the follow-up period.

Closed cases that were not re-referred

The following provides examples of two cases that did not result in a
re-referral to children's social care. The first case had been originally referred
by the adult learning disability team prior to the birth of the baby. The assessment resulted in a co-ordinated multi-agency plan for services. The review
suggests that improvements in parenting capacity had resulted from the provision of services, and that continued support from adult services and universal
services for children would ensure the child's continuing safety and welfare.

CARL, NEWBORN

Carl (see p.25 and p.53) lives with his mother who has learning disabilities
and his father who has poor mental health. The social worker explains that the
case came to the attention of children's social care because:

> There were concerns about mother's parenting skills and how she would
> cope with Carl. She has quite a severe learning disability and had been
> involved with a learning disability team for some time.

An initial and core assessment were carried out and there was multi-agency involvement in the Child in Need Plan. The resulting services included:

- parenting programme
- family care three times a week to help mother with routines, hygiene, home conditions, house-keeping skills
- family care worker to accompany mother when she went out to do things like shopping as she was very nervous with strangers
- social work support
- health visiting support
- assessment by clinical psychologist.

The comments of the family care worker suggest the services were having a positive impact although it was recognised that support would need to continue.

> I think that the agencies worked very well together and I worked closely with the health visitor in helping mum to feed the baby with appropriate foods. We developed a feeding programme... Mum does respond to our input. I am now going into the family three days a week for a two-hour session each of these days. This is quite a high level of input. I am mainly looking now at hygiene and safety and I hope this involvement will continue long term.

The need for continued support was also noted in the social worker's closure record.

> As Carl continues to develop mum may struggle with various aspects. This may especially be the case regarding application of guidance and boundaries, and possible play and stimulation issues. Hopefully this can be dealt with by universal services such as health visitor, but additional support/co-ordination may be needed. Additionally one possible re-emergent factor could be deterioration in household conditions. The involvement of adult services is necessary in this area as experience of working with adult learning disabilities is crucial to the success of any work around this. Support service to continue to be offered to the family especially by adult services for mum. Continued monitoring/support by universal services.

At the point of follow-up no further referral had been made to children's social care.

> [The case notes record] Paternal grandmother very involved and supportive. Gives general day to day support and cares for Carl about once a week for the day which gives mum a break.

referred because of concerns about Owen's care and welfare. At the time Owen's mother described the difficulties she was experiencing.

> I was having problems with Owen, I couldn't cope. I wanted them to put him in care for a bit. I just could not cope with him. His behaviour was hard. He never stays still. He won't be still for long. I was getting depressed and on pills for depression. I wanted him to go into foster care. I had been in care for a long time, until I was 16 or 17. I wanted help with him. I really wanted him to be in care and give me a break. (Researcher's interview with mother)

As a result of the Child in Need Plan Owen and his mother attended the family centre and work was directed at helping her to address a number of parenting issues, including Owen's general care, safety, stimulation, nutrition and feeding. Owen's mother also attended group sessions on parenting at the family centre. The health visitor continued to be involved with the family and provided general support and advice.

During the follow-up period Owen's parents separated. Owen's mother established a relationship with a young man whom she knew from her childhood in care. Another baby was born but the couple soon separated. The next referral to children's social care was made from a member of the public who wished to remain anonymous. The referral record notes her concerns.

> She says the children are being neglected and the mother puts her own needs before that of the children. Mother buys mobile phone top-up cards, cigarettes, and alcohol before milk and nappies, etc. The referrer added that mother allows strange men into the house and sleeps with them.

In response to the referral a visit was made to the home where a family friend was found to be looking after the children while Owen's mother collected her benefit money. The social worker recorded her observations on the visit.

> On arrival Owen was downstairs in the living room which was furnished and not clean to acceptable standards and very untidy. The door of the living room was off its hinges and three nails were protruding. Owen was not dressed and wearing trainer pants. The friend stated that he was not potty trained (he was almost three at time of this visit). Owen appears overweight for his age and his feet were filthy as though he had been playing in the garden without shoes on his feet. His body was clean. He was smiley and engaged with ourselves. There were age appropriate toys available.
>
> Edward (younger brother) was upstairs in his cot and crying. The friend went to get him. There was a loud crash and the friend said that she had tripped and nearly fallen in the cot, and spoke of the bedroom door being unsafe. We felt that her explanation was not a true version of events as

Edward had a small red mark on left side of his head, not substantial. In our opinion the friend had dropped him. Neither child had any bruising. We left our names and contact cards and asked that mother contact us. (Social worker's report found on case file)

A meeting was held at the family centre and the following plan established.

Family centre to provide intensive support in safety, cooking, dietary advice, establishing routines. Introduction to Sure Start scheme and encouragement for mother to attend a counselling course to address issues re. her past. She is to be introduced to a 'well women' clinic for advice about her own health. Permission was also given by mother to speak to the children's father in order to discuss how he can support the family effectively. Currently he just attends the house when he wants and does not take the children out. He constantly runs her down, which is an added burden to her. Mother advised us that she hopes to move house very soon as she finds the pressure of having other young people visiting her home too much. (Notes from the meeting at family centre held on the social worker's case file)

Following the meeting at the family centre and the agreement on the Child in Need Plan, the case was closed once again to children's social care. This case shows the difficulties agencies have in providing on-going day-to-day support that many parents with learning disabilities need. Owen's mother did not have the advantage of a partner without learning disabilities, an able parent or other adult relative to provide continuing support, advice and guidance to ensure Owen's and Edward's safety and welfare were being promoted.

Open cases

In ten instances the cases remained open to children's social care throughout the study period. In six cases the child had learning difficulties: in one instance the child lived in a shared care arrangement, looked after by his mother and foster carers, and in the other five the child was receiving on-going respite care. The other open cases involved four children from the same family who had been exposed to domestic violence and at the point of follow-up were living with their mother in a refuge. All the cases are highly complex and frequently had a long history of intermittent support from children's social care. In many ways they resemble the sample of cases that were re-referred during the study in that the parents lacked intensive support from relatives. Peter provides an example of a case that remained open to children's social care during the study period.

PETER, AGED 16 YEARS

The social work case file informs us that Peter lives with his parents, both of whom have learning disabilities. Peter himself has severe learning difficulties, has been diagnosed as autistic and presents challenging behaviour. He is extremely aggressive when in a temper.

It was noted on the case file that a large amount of family support and social worker intervention had been provided in the past. The referral at the first stage of the current study came from the hospital following treatment for an injury to Peter's leg. Concerns related to his parents' capacity to manage his post-operative care. There was also a request made by Peter's school for social work intervention because the parents were experiencing difficulties managing his behaviour.

The referral resulted in an assessment for 'transition to adulthood'. This noted that 'frequent supervision assistance will be required'. It was noted on the case file that Peter was to continue to receive respite care via a specialist home for young people with learning difficulties. A psychological assessment via the Child and Adolescent Mental Health Services (CAHMS) team was offered but refused by the family. At the point of follow-up the social work case file shows that respite care was continuing to be provided to the family although this was regularly reviewed to ensure it met the parents' needs.

> There is a plan drawn up for this [respite care] every six months – parents are asked what they would like – social services then endeavour to meet parents' requests.
>
> No pattern to the care – some five-day, some three-day respite care. E.g. in Dec 2004 it appears he had seven nights of respite care and in Jan 2005 nine nights of respite care. Respite starts at 4 pm until 10 am. (Recording taken from the social work case file)

The case file also provides insights into Peter's development and the direct support that is being provided to help him achieve his potential.

> Peter left school in July 2003 and is now attending a day resource centre to improve his general living skills, self care skills and to moderate his behaviour... The purpose is to increase his involvement in community activities and daily living skills. We are also willing to help where we can in supporting him in his health needs. Peter will not reach his potential in life as his parents are unable/unwilling to work with Peter. (Recording taken from the social work case file)

Developmental progress and circumstances of children who continued to live with their parents

The exploration of the progress of children who continued to live with parents with learning disabilities was by definition confined to the cases where there was both baseline data and current information. A social work assessment carried out at the first stage of the research provided the baseline data; information on children's current position was drawn either from a social worker's review or re-assessment (carried out within the follow-up year), or from an initial assessment conducted by a member of the research team.

In a number of cases information was only available at one point, and these have had to be excluded from this stage of the analysis, thus reducing the follow-up group to 31. For example, it was only possible to gather information, either from the case file or through carrying out an assessment, on the progress of 36 of the 52 children who had continued to live with their parents. Unfortunately, the sample was further reduced because in five of these cases no assessment had been carried out when children first came to the attention of children's social care – there were no baseline data.

Children's development over time

The initial assessment (discussed in Chapter 2) showed a high proportion of the children referred to children's social care who were living with a parent with learning disabilities had developmental needs. For example, approximately half the original group (51.8%) of children living with parents with learning disabilities were classified as having severe developmental needs. It will be recalled that children were classified as having severe developmental needs when the assessment identified needs in relation to three or more of the following areas: health, education, emotional and behavioural development, identity and social presentation, family and social relationships and self-care skills.

Although the profile of the group changed over time – some children had fewer problems while for others difficulties increased – the most prevalent pattern was for situations to endure. An exploration of the follow-up group shows the greatest level of continuing developmental need related to children's education, emotional and behavioural development, and health. For example, 12 of the 15 children (80%) identified as having educational needs at the first assessment continued to have educational needs at the point of follow-up as the following case illustrates.

ROGER, AGED SEVEN YEARS

Roger lives with his mother who has a learning disability, his stepfather, his sister aged 17 years and his two younger half siblings – Robbie aged nine years (see p.75) and Lucy aged six years. The family has been known to children's social care for approximately 12 years. With regard to Roger there had been concerns about his health and development and his mother's capacity to meet his needs since his birth. For example, when he was less than a year old the case notes record '…concerns regarding Roger's development…Roger not attending crèche due to Mum forgetting to take him'. At the age of seven years the school referred Roger with the following concerns, 'Roger teased at school, because of soiling'.

At the first stage of the study the social worker noted, in relation to 11-year-old Roger's education, that he was:

> Bright and intelligent and should achieve well but lacks encouragement. He is missing lessons and is frequently late for school. Recently excluded for three days for persistent refusal of school discipline.

To address these concerns and prevent the difficulties from escalating, Roger was provided with a learning mentor. Three years later at the point of the follow-up, Roger's educational difficulties were still evident as his mother explains.

> Roger says he doesn't like school and sometimes will not go. I tell him I don't want to go to prison because he will not go to school. Julian [stepfather] can be a bit hard on him and shouts and sends him to bed early if he will not go to school. I don't think he is happy at school and he doesn't have friends there. He doesn't like the teachers.

During the study period no re-referrals concerning Roger had been made to children's social care and the case remained closed to this organisation.

Similarly, continuing needs were identified for 15 of 19 children (78.9%) in relation to their emotional and behavioural development and 17 of 22 children (77.3%) in relation to their health, as the following case illustrates.

CATHY, AGED 15 YEARS

Cathy lives with her mother who has a learning disability. Cathy's older sister no longer lived at home. The family have been known to the adult learning disability team and to children's social care since Cathy's birth. The relationship between mother and daughter was reported to have been volatile. The worker for adult services explained their earlier concerns about Cathy.

There were child protection issues around neglect, poor feeding and dirty and unsafe home circumstances… When Cathy was aged about 13 she made accusations of being sexually abused by one of her mother's partners. The accusations were investigated but not substantiated.

During the follow-up period a further referral to children's social care had been made. The case file shows that a fracas between Cathy and her mother had resulted 'in mother hitting Cathy on the leg with an iron bar'. The mother was arrested but released without charge as Cathy did not wish to make a complaint. An initial assessment was completed and a social work service provided aimed at supporting the mother in managing Cathy's behaviour, and working with Cathy to address her behavioural and health needs. It was acknowledged that her sexual health was a cause for concern as the case notes indicate.

> Cathy has little knowledge of sex and contraception. Has previously received treatment for two sexually transmitted diseases. Cathy's understanding of her own health and safety is limited and her mother appears to have a similar low understanding.

Cathy who was just 18 years old at the point of follow-up, explains the issues from her perspective.

> My stepfather was sexually assaulting me. He touched me up from 6 years to 14 years. He raped me up the back passage. My mother would not believe me. I reported him to the police but nothing happened. He was also touching up my sister. My mum would not believe us. I wanted my mum to believe me but she loved him that much that she wouldn't.

She describes her health at the present time.

> I am not that well. I have epilepsy and asthma, and I have throat problems. I am not on medication but I want to be. I smoke and drink. I don't eat proper meals. My sister and friends give me something. I have taken drugs in the past, and I use contraceptive injections. But my sister thinks I am pregnant, I've got a bump in my tummy. I don't know if I am pregnant. I haven't seen a doctor. I haven't got a boyfriend any more. He was 24 and I saw him for three years. He treated me like a pig, he wanted a baby but I wasn't ready. I hope I am not pregnant, but we will see.

Cathy's mother's account reinforces this picture of poor health.

> Cathy doesn't eat nothing I make her, she drinks and takes drugs and gets drunk and hits me. I have been to hospital because she hit me in the eye and it isn't right still…her head's gone.

A Child in Need Plan was drawn up to address a number of issues where there were concerns. With regard to Cathy's health, provision was made for her to attend a young person's clinic where she was tested for sexually transmitted diseases. Following the initial assessment and the subsequent referral to the young person's clinic and rather unsuccessful attempts to encourage school attendance the case was closed once more to children's social care.

The information from the social work case notes on Cathy illustrates the long-term consequences of child abuse and neglect, and again shows the short-comings of targeted, time-limited interventions for children who live with parents with learning disabilities who do not have the support of other relevant, safe adults.

Although not as high, the rate of continuing needs was also of concern in relation to other aspects of children's development. For example, in over half the cases (15/27, 55.6%) children's needs in relation to family and social relationships continued and in 44.4 per cent of cases (8/18) needs continued to be present in relation to children's identity.

Focusing on those children whose needs continue should not obscure the fact that for some children earlier difficulties were no longer evident at the point of follow-up. For example, in some 20 per cent of cases educational, health and emotional and behavioural needs were no longer present. Even greater progress was found in relation to family and social relations and identity where approximately half the children no longer had needs at the point of follow-up.

Unfortunately, while some children improved, for others developmental needs became apparent as they became older. In particular, needs emerged in relation to education (noted now in an additional six cases), identity (in an additional five cases) and health (in an extra four cases). In only two cases were new needs noted in relation to emotional and behavioural needs or family and social relationships.

SEVERE DEVELOPMENTAL NEEDS OVER TIME

Twenty-three children (74.2%) were identified as having severe developmental needs at the first assessment and 17 (54.8%) at the point of follow-up. An examination of the data shows continuity was the most common pattern: children identified as having severe developmental needs at stage one were likely to continue to be so classified; over two-thirds (69.6%, 16/23) continued to meet the criteria. Just over half these cases (n=9) had been open to children's social care throughout the study period and were in receipt of on-going support and services. The remaining eight cases had been closed; two had been re-referred and additional help had been provided before they were closed once again. In the remaining six cases a Child in Need Plan had been developed for the child that identified the need for continuing services to be provided by agencies other than children's social care.

It is encouraging to find that the direction of change in relation to children's behavioural needs was positive. Practically one-third of the children (30.4%, 7/23) originally classified as showing severe developmental needs were no longer eligible, while only one child's development deteriorated to the extent of being classified as having severe needs at the point of follow-up.

Parents' capacity to meet their child's needs over time

The initial assessment (Chapter 2) revealed that the parents of over half (57%) the 56 children involved in the first part of the research were experiencing difficulties in meeting their children's needs in relation to three or more of the following issues: basic care, ensuring safety, emotional warmth, stimulation, guidance and boundaries, and stability.

The issue of enduring circumstances, identified in relation to children's developmental needs, also applied to most aspects of parenting. Parents who adequately met particular aspects of their children's needs at the first assessment were likely to continue to do so, and those experiencing difficulties were also likely to continue to struggle.

An examination of the various parenting dimensions shows the capacity to provide children with stability was a particularly problematic aspect of parenting: 14 of the 19 parents (73.7%) assessed as not providing their children with adequate stability at stage one continued to experience difficulties at the point of follow-up. Moreover, in over half the cases difficulties in parenting continued with respect to emotional warmth (60%), basic care (56%) and guidance and boundaries (53.8%). The following serves as an example of a child whose parents continued to experience difficulties in ensuring her safety and basic care for practically the whole two-year study period, despite the numerous agencies working with the family.

KATIE, AGED FOUR YEARS

Katie and her younger half sister live with her mother and stepfather, both of whom have learning disabilities (see p.59 and p.68). Katie's parents were in the care system as children and attended special schools. The referral at the time of the first assessment was as a result of an allegation made by four-year-old Katie that her stepfather had sexually abused her. Although children's social care decided not to pursue the allegation of sexual abuse, concerns about inconsistent parenting and her parents' capacity to protect her adequately triggered a core assessment.

> Concerns were noted about Katie being very friendly with comparative strangers, they [the parents] stated that this is a concern to them both.

As a result of the assessment a number of agencies worked with the family, including the health visiting service, children's social care, Sure Start, and a parent and toddler group. At the point of follow-up Katie was seven years old and concerns about her parents' capacity to meet her need for basic care continued as the social worker's report shows.

> Mum acknowledges that she has failed to protect Katie. Katie's recent sexualised behaviour coincides with mum disclosing that Katie's stepfather and grandfather have had unsupervised contact with her. When Katie has disclosed concerns regarding her grandfather mum has not believed her. Mum presents as very confused regarding her responsibility to ensuring her children's safety. During discussion mum said that she did not think Katie had been abused by her stepfather, but she acknowledged that she had placed Katie at risk by allowing the unsupervised contact. Mum is aware of the risk she has placed Katie in. However, she has allowed her father and Katie's stepfather to influence her about contact.
>
> Mum is experiencing difficulties in managing Katie's behaviour. Mum has disclosed that on some occasions she has hurt Katie. Mum admitted to hitting her and kicking her. Mum's friend explains that on one occasion she saw Katie coughing blood after she had been kicked. Mum is keen to accept support in caring for the children. Mum appears to be experiencing significant emotional and psychological difficulties at this time. There are significant concerns regarding mum's failure to protect and to meet the children's needs.

The outcome of an initial assessment was that Katie was accommodated under section 20 of the Children Act 1989 (voluntary accommodation) and the family centre were working with Katie. The latest report provides some insight into the outcome.

> Children have settled very well into foster placement and new school. Contact is currently twice a week, however this needs further dealing with. Mum is to have more contact during school holidays – needs arranging. Looks like this case needs to go into proceedings. Very concerning that Katie keeps making allegations against men of a sexual nature, however family centre is doing some work on this.

Some aspects of parenting, however, appeared to be more open to change. In over half the cases parenting improved in relation to meeting the child's needs for stimulation (58.3%) and safety (56%).

Continuity in positive parenting was also true in relation to stability: all ten parents originally assessed as providing adequate stability for their children continued to be so classified at the point of follow-up. Continuity was also high in relation to emotional warmth where in two-thirds of cases (12 of 18) parents continued to meet their child's needs adequately. Although the numbers are too small to analyse, the pattern of continuity also applied to the other aspects of parenting.

SEVERE PARENTING DIFFICULTIES OVER TIME

The direction of change was most obvious when considering cases where parents had been classified as experiencing severe difficulties in relation to their parenting capacity. It was possible to follow up 28 cases, half of which still met the criteria for severe difficulties – 14 had improved. Of the 14 cases where difficulties in parenting capacity continued, eight had remained open to children's social care during the study period. Of the six closed cases only one was the subject of a re-referral. Once again the numbers of cases not classified as showing severe difficulties at the first assessment were very small and no analysis was possible. The findings suggest that over time and with the intervention of services in half the cases parents were able to improve their parenting.

The following case notes provide the context for four children from the same family (see p.75 and p.88). They were written by the member of the research team carrying out the second assessment, and provide an example of parents who are experiencing severe difficulties in parenting all their children. The family at the time of the follow-up included the parents and their children: Jean, 19 years, her brother Roger, 13 years, and their half siblings, Robbie, aged 9 years who is autistic and his sister Lucy, aged 6 years. The case notes show the complexity of the case and the many challenges facing these parents. The case was originally referred to children's social care by the school who noticed cigarette burns on Robbie's foot. Robbie's father, who had been responsible for the injury, was asked to leave the family home temporarily. At the review it was agreed he should return home 'so that there could be some stability'.

> The interview took place in the family home, a four-bedded council house on a large estate. The area did not look rundown, and the one room we saw,

the front main room, was clean and newly decorated by Roger's stepfather and was warm and pleasant. Roger's mother, a short, large lady, lay down on the couch for most of the interview. She presented as a dis-inhibited lady. The first thing she said to me was to direct me to a chair opposite her as she didn't want me near her bare feet, which she indicated smelled. There was no embarrassment when she said this. She and her husband Julian are both clearly learning disabled, but were able to articulate their views and feelings very well.

The mother admitted to drinking too much and frequently wakes with hangovers. She drinks mostly in the house. She has some health problems and stated she gets regular dizzy spells and blackouts, following which she has to lie down for a period. These do not seem to have been medically diagnosed. She does not like her GP, whom she says is reluctant to treat any member of the family.

The stepfather said very little and was reluctant to talk about his family background. He would appear to have a bad temper from what his wife said, although this was not in any way evident during the interview.

There were many indications of a family facing many tensions and problems. Robbie [aged 9 years] is severely disabled, having been diagnosed with autism, unable to speak, doubly incontinent and needing constant care. He irritates the other children with his noises and regular hand clapping. Robbie needs changes of clothing on a daily basis and still uses nappies both during the day and night. Fortunately, Robbie has respite care two days every week, and this seems to be a major support for the family.

The behaviour of Lucy [6 years] is of some concern. She goes around the house undressed, and in her mother's words, 'lifts her legs in the air'. Roger and Lucy have a poor relationship. His mother explains that he was 'lashing out at her, and jumping on top of her, sometimes until she can't breathe, and has to be pulled off'. Mum also said that Lucy is very vulnerable outside the home as she will approach men in cars and talk to them. She has been warned of the dangers of this but continues to behave in this way. She has also been warned about her behaviour in school where at least one incident is reported of her pulling down the trousers of a boy in the class. Mum was warned that if this behaviour continued Lucy would be required to leave the school.

Roger exhibits difficult behaviour, apparently bordering on the violent, both within the house and in the street. He mixes with friends who smoke and make a nuisance of themselves, frequently knocking on the front door of another boy and refusing to stop. This causes distress to his mother as Julian [stepfather] reacts by screeching at the boy and threatening him, and mum is afraid that there will be trouble with the boy's parents.

> The oldest child, Jean, has recently been thrown off a course she was attending at the local college because of very bad time keeping and not turning up at all. She stays in bed until the afternoon on most days, refusing to get up.

Although the family were experiencing myriad difficulties, nonetheless the researcher's concluding remarks were not totally negative.

> Despite all of their problems, the family are together and coping in a sort of way. The only service they are currently receiving is respite care for Robbie.

Family and environmental factors over time

The findings from the initial assessment (discussed in Chapter 2) suggest that family and environmental factors (issues such as family history and functioning, social resources, housing and employment, and income) pose the greatest challenge to children living with parents with learning disabilities. Of the 56 children involved in the initial stage of the research, two-thirds were in families assessed as experiencing severe difficulties with family and environmental factors (two or more of the four areas assessed as inadequate).

The area of family history and functioning continued to bedevil children and their families. Of the 26 cases where this had been identified as a problem at the first assessment, all but one (96.2%) continued to experience difficulties. The following cases illustrate the difficulties identified at the point of follow-up.

FRED, AGED THREE YEARS

Fred lives with his mother Amanda (see p.75). The social worker's recent report shows the continuing impact that family issues were having. The case remained open to children's social care throughout the study period.

> It is thought that Amanda [mother] was sexually abused as a child and it appears that she had periods in care. As an adult she has been the subject of domestic violence on a number of occasions and involving different males. She has moved home on numerous occasions before settling down in her current accommodation in May last year. Fred has had no direct involvement with his father since he was 18 months old, and Fred does not ask about his father. These issues are causing mum concern and stress.

Housing was the other area where shortcomings appeared to be most impervious to change. At the first assessment 21 children were living in housing assessed as inadequate, and of these 16 (76.2%) continued to live in unsuitable housing. Moreover, for a further five children housing circumstances deteriorated, resulting in them being classed as inadequate at the point of follow-up.

FRANK, AGED NINE YEARS

Frank lives with his parents (both of whom have a learning disability) and his seven siblings, all of whom have learning difficulties (see social worker's report on p.69). The review illustrates the housing difficulties facing the family.

> Family live in a council house which is in a rural and isolated area. The accommodation is too small to meet their needs, particularly the sons who all share a room and a bed.

The case was closed and following a further referral closed again to children's social care. The closure report noted the reason for closure. It is of interest that the housing difficulties were not mentioned.

> With help and guidance from various agencies the family have become independent. Family care withdrew their services three months ago and the family have managed extremely well without this extra help. We feel that Alan [dad] is capable of looking after his family now without input from the local authority.

The social work record provides insights into what happened to the family in the subsequent months and their continuing progress.

> Since the case has been closed Mother has left/thrown out of the family home and is now living with her mother. The children are now being cared for by dad and a 16-year-old girl who has moved in. She appears to be supporting dad in the care of the eight children. Mum comments that she [16-year-old girl] is good at looking after the children.
>
> [The health visitor comments] I saw dad and Katy [16-year-old girl], all the school children were still in their uniforms as they hadn't been home long and I must say it is the cleanest and tidiest I have ever seen them. Their hair was clean and shiny and free from head lice and they all had the right size uniform on.

Although the current situation suggests that the children are being adequately cared for, the challenge of looking after eight children all of whom have some degree of learning difficulties is likely to overwhelm a father with learning disabilities even if he has the support of a 16-year-old girl. The findings suggest that this family need continuing support from a number of agencies including housing.

PETER, AGED 16 YEARS

Peter (see pp.85–86) lives with his parents and his younger sister, all of whom have learning disabilities. The most recent case review discussed the housing difficulties faced by the family.

> The family live in an isolated rural area and neither mum nor dad can drive. There is limited public transport which creates a problem in them accessing services. They have asked for a change of house but nothing has happened on this.

The result of the review was that transport was funded by children's social care to allow Peter to attend the day resource centre, respite care and other services. The case remained open to children's social care throughout the study period.

Some families were themselves able to address specific aspects of their housing problems as demonstrated by the following case.

SUSAN, AGED EIGHT YEARS

Susan (see p.79) lives with her mother (who has a learning disability), her father and her younger brother. The child protection review shows the resourcefulness of some families.

> The family live in a three bed council house. On occasions it has become shabby and poorly decorated but dad does his best to keep it maintained and has recently solved the problem of mum washing the lounge carpet with a mop – by laying a laminate floor.

Following a review, which took account of the father's efforts, the case was closed.

The areas where children's circumstances were most likely to show some improvement were social resources (issues such as relationships with the wider family and the community, and the use of local resources) and family income. For example, although 16 of the 28 children (57.1%) continued to live in families where social resources were inadequate, and for an additional two cases adequate circumstances deteriorated, this should not mask the finding that for 12 (42.9%) children things improved.

Family income showed the greatest degree of positive change. Of the 24 children living in households where income was considered to be inadequate at the first assessment, things improved for 17 (70.8%). In only seven cases had income continued to be inadequate and in a further two cases a positive situation deteriorated. The following serve as examples of how family members and agency workers helped families to resolve their financial difficulties.

JONATHAN, AGED FOUR YEARS

Jonathan has learning difficulties and behavioural problems and lives with his parents. The social worker's report describes the financial difficulties facing the family and how these were resolved.

> Mum has been calculated as having debts of over £8000. She sought advice from the Citizens Advice Bureau who suggested that she goes bankrupt and they have explained to her the implications of this. She is now going through the process of bankruptcy.

The case was closed to children's social care although they continued to receive some support from the learning disability team.

HARRY, AGED 15 YEARS

Harry lives with his mother and his older sister. Harry's mother describes the assistance she received from statutory agencies and from her extended family and how this helped her.

> They [adult services] helped me get a job as a lollipop lady. My father-in-law sorts out all my bills, and my brother-in-law. I don't have any debts. I did have but they have all been sorted out. (Researcher's interview with mother's report)

The case was closed to children's social care.

SEVERE DIFFICULTIES IN FAMILY AND ENVIRONMENTAL FACTORS OVER TIME

Severe difficulties in family and environmental factors were least accessible to change. Of the 29 cases originally assessed as experiencing severe difficulties, 27 (93.1%) were continuing to be so classified and an additional two cases fulfilled the criteria at the point of follow-up. Only three cases were not classified as experiencing severe difficulties in family and environmental factors at the point of follow-up, all of which were closed to children's social care. Of those that were experiencing severe difficulties in family and environmental factors 17 were closed to children's social care and 12 were open cases.

The continuity of severe difficulties in all three domains of children's lives – those categorised as experiencing multiple problems

When children were assessed as having severe developmental needs *and* parents were assessed as experiencing severe difficulties in parenting *and* there were severe difficulties in relation to family and environmental factors, cases were classed as having multiple problems. At the first assessment over half the 31 cases (n=18, 58.1%) fulfilled these criteria. Change was in a positive direction: at the point of follow-up 13 cases met the criteria (41.9%). However, there was much evidence of continuity. Of the 18 cases classed as experiencing multiple problems at the first assessment, over half (n=10, 55.6%) were similarly classified at the point of follow-up.

Eight of the 13 cases categorised as multiple problem cases at the point of follow-up had remained open to children's social care. It is of some concern that five cases were closed although there were severe needs in all three areas of children's lives. In two cases both children and parents had learning disabilities. All the cases had a long history of interventions from a range of different agencies including children's social care.

The findings suggest that the considerable input of services does not appear to bring about the required changes to the development and circumstances of some children. For example, the Tandy family (see p.32) had first been referred to children's social care nine years ago and has remained open ever since. New concerns over the years triggered fresh rounds of assessment and intervention. At the first stage of the research the family comprised the parents, both of whom have learning disabilities, and their children: Adam (two years), Emma (four years), Pamela (seven years), and Janice (eight years). The social worker explained the reason for the assessment.

> It was reported by the health visitor that the house was incredibly dirty, including dog dirt in a number of the rooms. The family also have quite large snakes in the front room, kept in a box. The children appeared not to be being fed properly. Dental and doctor appointments are not being kept. Dad is reported to be drinking very heavily and Mum has quite serious epilepsy and has regular seizures. She is not managing her medication appropriately and the collective picture is one of some concern. Mrs Tandy has a learning disability and she is difficult to understand. Mr Tandy is also learning disabled.

As a result of this assessment the family were re-housed, child minders were provided, social workers and health visitors offered support and the general practitioner was to review Mrs Tandy's medication. The researcher's report at the time of first interview (one year on) suggests that the services provided had not made a significant difference to the family's circumstances.

> Although they had moved from a flat to a house, the house was now extremely unkempt, dirty and smelly. Their dog, which is a large dog, was out of control but not really aggressive. The snake was in a box in the front room and the children were playing in that room. The father drinks very heavily, and the mother continues to suffer from uncontrolled epileptic fits.

During the follow-up period a family crisis had resulted in further changes for the family. Mrs Tandy recollects what triggered the latest flurry of activity.

> My husband started beating me up. He started in the night. He kept on through the night. I tried to get away but he wouldn't let me. He hurt me. The kids saw it, they were upset. He went to sleep and the next morning I went out. I went to the shops. I saw Margaret [a worker from Sure Start, with whom the family were involved] and she asked me what was wrong. I told her he'd beaten me up and she got hold of Brian [social worker]. I never went back home. Brian got me in here [the women's refuge] that day with the kids and I have been here till now… We had a snake and two dogs in the house but they said I couldn't bring them here, they wouldn't let me so someone has taken them.

If the chance meeting with the Sure Start worker had not occurred it is probable that Mrs Tandy would not have sought the assistance of any formal agency; she has no history of initiating help. Without their intervention one can only speculate what would have happened to this mother and her children. Mrs Tandy does not have the support of a partner, or of an extended family; the maternal grandparents are dead and the paternal grandparents live some considerable distance away and have little interest or contact with their grandchildren. She has no friends outside the women's hostel.

The follow-up assessment reveals that Mrs Tandy's health continues to be poor and this affects her capacity to carry out routine household tasks. Without her husband Mrs Tandy relies on her eldest daughter Janice (now aged ten years) to assume the main caring role.

> I take a lot of drugs for epilepsy, and they make me feel drunk, sleepy. Janice looks after me when I am not well. She is good, she cares for me. My husband was my carer but now Janice looks after me. Janice helps me when I have fits and with my drugs… I can do the washing and Janice helps. I could cook but mainly go out to McDonalds or to the fish and chip shop. Janice will help me when we go to the other house. I've got my own pans and things. Janice will help me keep the house clean when we go.

Mrs Tandy is aware of the impact her poor health is having on her capacity to look after her children.

> I can have a seizure any time. I could have one when I am speaking to you. Since I've been here it's getting worse. With taking my medication I feel worse. Feel like I am having blackouts. I can't remember what happened yesterday... I used to take the children to the park and feed the ducks, but I can't do that now because I might have a fit. I can't let them play on swings and things like that because I might have a fit. I have a hard time with them and keeping them from doing things. Sometimes I tell them to do things and they just run off, sometimes they are OK. Dad used to keep them under control but he's not here now. I'll never go back to him.

The plan is for the family to move to supported housing. The care worker at the women's refuge expressed satisfaction with the progress made by the family but is aware that they will need considerable support once they leave.

> It's going to be difficult when they get a home. They will need support when they leave here. There will be a warden available all day but at night there is a call system. Although they have done brilliantly since coming here the kids' behaviour is a problem. Janice can be very controlling and dominating. Janice will be the main problem. Managing all the kids will be a problem for mum.

The Tandy family illustrate the multiplicity of the difficulties experienced by children and parents with learning disabilities and the difficulties agencies and organisations face when trying to ensure the children are safeguarded and their welfare promoted. Janice will need support in her caring role as research has shown that young carers can experience substantial physical, emotional and social difficulties, and encounter problems in school and in relation to extra-curricular activities (Dearden and Becker 2002; SCIE 2005).

In many cases a considerable package of services, involving different agencies, was offered to families. Early identification enables practitioners to provide well-targeted services to families before major problems arise, and planned, time-limited interventions can successfully address the immediate issue.

However, short-term services for children living with a parent with learning disabilities have been shown to result in frustration and burnout on the part of the practitioner and mistrust, despair and recurrent crisis episodes for families. Training and support must be continued because as children grow up their needs change and they present different challenges to their parents (McGaw and Newman 2005). Continuing working relationships can result in greater mutual trust and respect, a maturation in the ways families use support, more prevention and early intervention, and opportunities for practitioners to develop a more holistic approach (McGaw 1996).

The findings from the current study suggest short-term packages of services did not generally meet the needs of the children and their parents. Unless there is continued informal and formal support and contingency planning, there is much evidence that these families lurch from one crisis to another, resulting each time in a new flurry of specific time-limited agency interventions. Moreover, the findings show that some cases were not subject to regular review and as a consequence children's progress and development were not monitored. There was considerable evidence to suggest that the welfare of a significant proportion of children was not being promoted and they were continuing to live in unacceptable situations. Social work practice in relation to regularly reviewing all children in receipt of social work services should be addressed with the implementation of the Integrated Children's System (www.everychildmatters.gov.uk/socialcare/integratedchildrenssystem/about/).

Summary

- The findings on the administrative and legal outcomes for children living with parents with learning disabilities are based on 64 cases; 12 cases were lost to the study.

- As a result of the intervention of children's social care 17.2 per cent of the sample was removed from the care of their parents. Two children were freed for adoption and nine children were continuously looked after for a period of at least one year.

- An examination of cases where children were removed from the care of their parents suggests the decision was not taken precipitately but only after a range of service provisions had failed to bring about the required changes. The broad age range of the children belies the widely held assumption that children's social care is likely to remove babies from the care of parents with learning disabilities.

- Fifty-two children continued to live with their parents. In two-thirds of cases all the adults in the household had a learning disability. One-third of the children lived in households that contained an adult, such as another parent or relative, who did not have a learning disability.

- Many children (n=29) themselves had one or more form of disability.

- In most cases (88.5%) no statutory orders applied to children living with parents with learning disabilities.

- During the three-year follow-up many children had undergone practical changes in their lives; 19 had moved house and 23 had experienced the arrival or departure of a key member of their household.

- When social work assessments of children identified developmental needs, or difficulties in parenting capacity or in relation to family and environmental factors, in most cases this resulted in some form of planned, targeted intervention. Social workers, however, did not routinely record whether the planned services had been forthcoming or the extent to which families had taken advantage of the proffered service.

- In the majority of cases (78.8%) children who had been referred to children's social care were no longer receiving a service from this agency at the point of follow-up (the case is closed). When cases had been closed (n=41), approximately half (n=23) were re-referred within the study period.

- The progress of individual children was confined to those where there was baseline data *and* current information, reducing the group to 31 cases.

- The most prevalent pattern was for difficulties to continue, regardless of the interventions of different agencies. For example, over three-quarters of children showing developmental needs with regard to their education, emotional and behavioural development and health at the time of the assessment, continued to have needs at the point of follow-up. A similar pattern of enduring difficulties was found in relation to parenting capacity and family and environmental factors.

- The pattern of enduring difficulties was also found in relation to children classified as experiencing multiple problems (severe developmental needs *and* severe difficulties in parenting *and* severe difficulties in relation to family and environmental factors). Half those originally classed as experiencing multiple problems continued to fulfil the criteria at the point of follow-up.

- Although there is a strong pattern of continuity, the direction of change is encouraging. In the majority of cases where change occurred this was in relation to reduced needs, improved parenting or fewer issues in relation to the wider family and environment.

- The findings suggest that children who were safeguarded and their welfare promoted lived in families where the parent with learning disabilities had the continuing day-to-day support of a capable non-abusive adult, such as a partner, relative or committed foster carer (a shared care arrangement), and were taking full advantage of universal and specialist services when necessary. When such committed support was not forthcoming children's changing needs were not met and they ricocheted between various statutory and voluntary agencies as concerns about their safety rose and fell with the changes in their circumstances and the impact of targeted, short-term interventions.

Chapter 5

Conclusions

The majority of parents want to do the best for their children. Whatever their circumstances or difficulties, the concept of partnership between the State and the family, in situations where families are in need of assistance in bringing up their children, lies at the heart of child care legislation. (Department of Health *et al.* 2000a, p.12, paragraph 1.44)

This fundamental principle underpins the Children Act 1989, the Assessment Framework (Department of Health 2000) and the Integrated Children's System (Department for Education and Skills 2006). In order to find out what is happening to a child, practitioners must develop open, honest and co-operative working relationships with parents or caregivers that ensure they feel respected and informed, and encourage them to feel confident in providing vital information about their child, themselves and their circumstances.

Research has shown that the implementation of the Assessment Framework has improved parents' understanding of the assessment process and increased their involvement at every stage (Cleaver *et al.* 2004). In cases where a child is living with parents with learning disabilities, social workers are just as committed to working in partnership and spend considerable time trying to ensure that they understand the purpose of the assessment, what it will involve and how long it will take. Parents' accounts, however, suggest that even social workers' best efforts do not always have the anticipated results. Although in every case social workers made great efforts to explain why they would be carrying out an assessment, practically one-third of parents with learning disabilities had difficulty remembering what had been said to them.

In many cases social workers reported that the parents' learning disability was an obstacle to their full involvement in the assessment process. Although most parents understood and could recall concrete aspects of the assessment, such as talking about their family dynamics, more complex issues, such as giving their consent to social workers to talk to other relevant professionals about them, proved more elusive.

Many parents with learning disabilities were eager to agree with whatever professionals said. Although social workers tried to ensure that they gained the true views of parents, they worried that this tendency towards acquiescence encouraged over-optimistic assumptions about the extent of parents' understanding and capacity to put agreed plans into practice. To balance this, social workers tended not to take parents' responses at face value.

Children who live with parents with learning disabilities account for only a small proportion of all children referred to children's social care. It would therefore be unrealistic to expect social workers from children and family teams to have the expertise and specialist skills needed to work with people with learning disabilities. To assist them in carrying out assessments that involved parents with learning disabilities, social workers used a number of different strategies to increase parents' understanding and involvement and to assess their parenting skills. These included:

- using a close relative or friend in interviews to act as an intermediary
- arranging for interviews to take place at the social work office to cut down the distractions and keep parents focused on the task in hand
- including other known professionals in meetings to reassure parents and put them at their ease
- arranging for families to attend family centres to help with the assessment of parents' capacity to develop and learn relevant parenting skills.

However, parents with learning disabilities can find family centres intimidating when they are in the minority, and workers may not have the expertise in working with adults with a learning disability.

There was little evidence of social workers in children and family teams making use of professionals with specialist skills in working with people with learning disabilities or taking advantage of relevant toolkits or questionnaires and scales aimed at assessing parenting skills. Not using specialist toolkits may reflect a lack of awareness of these materials, gaps in in-service training, and/or their availability to workers within children and family teams.

Collaboration between adult learning disability teams and children and family teams during the assessment of children and families was rare. Barriers to collaborative work included: the different thresholds for services; children's social workers not consulting workers in adult learning disability teams; parental reluctance to being involved with learning disability teams.

Referrals to children's social care that involved a parent with learning disabilities differed from other referrals. For example, parents rarely initiated the help; children were more likely to be under the age of five years; and a greater proportion of referrals were for concerns over the child's safety, parenting capacity, or the parent's learning disability.

Most referrals (89.5%) involving parents with learning disabilities resulted in social workers carrying out some form of assessment (either initial or core). These assessments showed that this group of children have significantly more needs than a comparison group. For example, initial assessments revealed that half (51.8%) the children living with a parent with learning disabilities had severe developmental needs (compared with one-third of the comparison group); in over half (57%) the cases severe parenting difficulties were identified (this applied to one-third of the comparison group); and in two-thirds (66.1%) of cases there were severe difficulties in relation to family and environmental factors (compared with 43.4% of the comparison group). Moreover, one-third of children living with a parent with learning disabilities had severe needs in all three domains, compared with 7.9 per cent of the comparison group. Although these children were more likely to have severe difficulties in all three domains of their lives, it is important not to pathologise all children living with a parent with learning disabilities. Nonetheless, the difficulties the children were facing should not be underestimated; all but six children (89.3%) had severe needs in at least one of the three domains.

The findings from the core assessment showed a similar but more extreme profile. In particular, children living with parents with learning disabilities were most disadvantaged in relation to family and environmental factors. The qualitative study showed families where a parent had learning disabilities were frequently experiencing severe poverty and were living in very inadequate housing. These issues may be exacerbated by the problems people with learning disabilities experience in managing budgets and accessing all their entitlements.

The core assessment showed that in most cases (91.3%) parents with learning disabilities were also experiencing other issues that negatively affected their ability to meet the needs of their children, such as poor mental and physical health, domestic violence, growing up in care, or substance misuse. The prevalence of co-morbidity for parents with learning disabilities has been well documented (McConnell and Llewellyn 2000). Moreover, many parents with learning disabilities have the added challenge of bringing up at least one child with learning disabilities, a high proportion of whom also have physical disabilities.

In only 2 of 76 cases did the assessment (initial or core) that involved a child living with a parent with learning disabilities result in no further action. However, ensuring parents with learning disabilities were aware of the outcome of the assessment and the details of the Child in Need Plan proved difficult. Practically one-third of parents were unaware of the plan.

When parents knew about the plan for their child and family they did not always agree with all aspects; only half the parents with learning disabilities agreed with every element. If parents disagreed with the plan or were dissatisfied with the assessment process, making an official complaint would have been difficult because at the time of the research local authorities did not have information about their complaints procedures or access to records available in a format accessible to people with learning disabilities.

The extent to which these parents were satisfied with the outcome of the assessment reflected the findings from the authors' larger study of assessments (Cleaver *et al.* 2004). Parental satisfaction was related to:

- parents and social workers having the same understanding of the reason for the assessment
- parents being involved in the assessment and planning
- parents agreeing with the plan
- the planned services being available.

Two years after the referral, local authorities could supply very limited information from their electronic records about the administrative outcomes. What was available suggests that children living with a parent with learning disabilities were significantly more likely than other children to:

- continue to receive a service from children's social care
- have parents who had received some services in their own right
- have had their name placed on the child protection register
- have become looked after.

A detailed follow-up of a group of 64 children of parents with learning disabilities three years after the original referral shows that the majority of children (83%) were living at home with their parent(s). The findings suggest that a key factor distinguishing children who remained living safely with their parents from those who did not show satisfactory progress and those who were removed was the presence of a non-abusive adult such as a partner or relative.

Of those children who were removed from the parents' care two had been freed for adoption and nine had been fostered for more than a year. There was no evidence to suggest that parental learning disability in itself was the reason children were removed. Removing children was very much a 'last resort'; the decision to place children away from home was taken after a substantial input of services had failed to bring about the necessary changes.

A similar degree of service input was identified in relation to children who remained living at home. For example, when social work assessments had identified children as having developmental needs, difficulties in relation to parenting capacity, or difficulties in relation to family and environmental factors, a targeted service was recorded on the Child in Need Plan. For example, an assessment identifying that a child had head lice resulted in a plan identifying the health visitor as the professional responsible for working with the mother to ensure the correct treatment was applied. However, information on the provision and take-up of services was not systematically recorded.

There was little evidence of plans to provide ongoing support and training for parents with learning disabilities to ensure they had the capacity to react appropriately to, for example, their child's changing health needs – an issue that was frequently left to chance. This was reflected by the finding that in most cases the involvement of children's social care was time-limited. Three years after the referral the majority of cases (78.8%) were closed to children's social care. At this point families were dependent on universal services for support and advice in bringing up their children, although in a very limited number of cases (3 out of 52) parents were receiving support from learning disability teams within adult services.

The policy of short-term interventions resulted in cyclical crisis episodes for families; over half the cases closed to children's social care were re-referred at least once within three years. Moreover, half the children who continued to live with their parents had their names placed on the child protection register during this time. For practically a quarter of these children (24%) this was not the first time their names had featured on the authority's child protection register.

Despite a wide range of services being provided to families following a referral to children's social care, on the whole these were targeted at addressing specific issues. Some aspects of children's safety and welfare were not adequately addressed and the overwhelming pattern was for high levels of need to continue. For example, over three-quarters of children originally assessed as having educational, emotional and behavioural and health needs continued to have needs at the point of follow-up. A similar pattern of enduring difficulties was found in relation to parenting capacity and family and environmental factors.

Of particular concern was the finding that the pattern of enduring difficulties was also evident for children with the greatest needs. Over half the children classified as experiencing multiple problems (severe developmental needs *and* severe difficulties in parenting *and* severe difficulties in relation to family and environmental factors) were in a similar situation three years later.

Although there was a strong trend towards continuity, it must be acknowledged that when changes did occur they were generally positive. For example, in a limited number of cases children displayed fewer developmental needs, difficulties in relation to parenting capacity had improved, and factors within the family and environment had been addressed.

Short-term, targeted interventions by statutory and voluntary agencies, on their own, were not sufficient to address the needs of children living with parents with learning disabilities. Unless there is continued informal and formal support and contingency planning these families tend to lurch from one crisis to another. Moreover, the findings suggest that some cases were not subject to regular review and as a consequence the children's progress and development were not monitored. To ensure children are safe and their welfare is promoted this intensity of support will be needed for the duration of their childhood. When such committed support was not forthcoming children's safety and welfare were not promoted and they ricocheted between a variety of statutory and voluntary agencies.

Implications for policy and practice

- Social workers are committed to working in partnership with parents with learning disabilities. However, more needs to be done to enable parents to feel competent and become involved in the assessment and plans for their children. Local authorities should, therefore, ensure that:

- ∘ information about assessments and services is available in a format that is easily accessible to people with learning disabilities (for example, Easy Read versions, information on CD/DVD, accessible websites, or speaking directly to parents or would-be parents who have learning disabilities)

- ∘ practitioners in children's services are aware of the resources available for working with parents with learning disabilities

- ∘ practitioners in children's services have access to experts who have specialist skills in communicating and working with people with learning disabilities, such as workers in adult learning disability teams, voluntary groups, or a knowledgeable 'mentor' within their own team

- ∘ local authority training programmes cover how best to support parents with learning disabilities to parent their children

- ∘ managers regularly audit and monitor training in order to identify gaps and plan future courses.

- There was little evidence of collaborative work between adult and children's services despite the raft of government guidance supporting joint working and information sharing (for example, *Every Child Matters* (Cm 5860 2003); the *National Service Framework for Children* (Department of Health and Department for Education and Skills 2004); *Every Child Matters: Change for Children* (HM Government 2004); *Working Together to Safeguard Children* (HM Government 2006a) and the Integrated Children's System, www.everychildmatters.gov.uk/socialcare/integratedchildrenssystem/about). Greater priority should be given to the involvement of adult services and other relevant voluntary and community services at the assessment and planning stage. This involvement will provide a more holistic understanding of the child's needs and the level of family functioning and is likely to encourage a more proactive approach to the delivery of services.

- Different thresholds for services and the diverse legal and ethical considerations hampered collaboration. Local authorities should establish protocols and procedures to ensure adult services and children's social care work collaboratively with children in need and their parents who have learning disabilities.

- Attention should be given to exploring whether grants from the Independent Living Fund could be used to help adults with learning disabilities with childcare costs or to support needs that relate to parenting a child.

- Inter-agency and interdisciplinary training on the Assessment Framework and the Integrated Children's System should ensure that professionals working in adult services are fully involved. The historically low priority that adult services have given to ensuring the wellbeing of their clients' dependent children must change.

- Children who live with a parent with learning disabilities and are referred to children's social care have high levels of need. To ensure the needs of individual children are met, careful attention must be given to each child within the family during the process of assessment, planning and review. Family-based assessments and plans, and the cloning of information between the records of children within the same family, were not uncommon at the time of the study. Such practices are not in line with the requirements of the Assessment Framework and can all too easily result in the needs of particular children not being identified or addressed appropriately.

- Social work assessments that involve children living with parents with learning disabilities generally result in a range of planned services to support the family. Reviewing and recording whether the planned service has resulted in the anticipated intervention is essential if the factors affecting children's developmental progress are to be fully understood. Line managers should ensure that recording practice is in line with government guidance. The implementation of the Integrated Children's System should enable social workers' recording practice to be more easily monitored.

- In most cases service provision is time-limited and targeted at addressing specific needs. A long-term package of services will be necessary to meet the diverse and enduring, complex and multiple needs of families where a parent or parents have learning disabilities. Resources must be committed for the duration of these children's childhood. Local authorities need to take account of the continuing demands on services and resources required to ensure the welfare of these children is safeguarded and promoted.

- When parents do not have the day-to-day support of a caring, safe adult, such as a partner or relative, no single agency will be able to provide all the services and support necessary to keep children safe and improve their wellbeing while living at home. These children are the responsibility of everyone and innovative approaches should be explored which may include both formal service provision and support, alongside the mobilisation of wider family networks and community-based services. These could include supported housing, family tenancies, child and adult foster care, open adoption, shared parenting and using volunteer parent mentors. Services provided by statutory agencies should be closely integrated with less formal networks of support.

- Intervention should be on-going and organised in such a way that parents are enabled to feel competent. Services should supplement and support existing resources and strengths within the family and community and include parents and children in solving their own problems so that they feel they have control over events in their lives.

- Greater use should be made of training programmes geared towards individual parents' learning patterns. An effective approach is for a children's services practitioner working together with a colleague who has the expertise in learning disability to deliver training to parents within their own home.

- It is essential that in every case the impact of services on children's developmental needs and circumstances is regularly reviewed. The implementation of the Integrated Children's System (www.everychildmatters.gov.uk/socialcare/integratedchildrenssystem/about) will support a process of systematic reviews of services provided and outcomes achieved. Currently the research suggests that the provision of services is not always successful in improving the outcomes for these children and some may be left in circumstances that are likely to impair their emotional and physical health and place them at risk of significant harm. Greater vigilance and more careful assessment and analysis of children's needs is required to determine what it is that has to change to improve outcomes for children and whether this is happening.

Definitions, Aims and Methods

Defining learning disability

The Department of Health (Cm 5086 2001) publication, *Valuing People*, states that learning disability includes the presence of:

- a significantly reduced ability to understand new or complex information, to learn new skills (impaired intelligence), with

- a reduced ability to cope independently (impaired social functioning)

- which started before adulthood, with a lasting effect on development.

(Cm 5086 2001, p.14, paragraph 1.5)

Valuing People groups people with learning disabilities into those with mild/moderate learning disabilities and those with severe and profound learning disabilities. Parents with any degree of learning disability were included in this study.

The decision to include a case within the study sample was taken based on evidence contained in the case file. A member of the research team scrutinised the case file to ensure the parent fell within the Department of Health's definition of learning disability. For example, cases were included when professionals had recorded on the case file that the parent had learning disabilities and/or the case file showed that the parent had been, or was, receiving services from an adult learning disability service. As a result, in order to ensure the criteria for learning disability were met, some documentation other than the referral must have been held on the case file. The following is an illustration of information recorded on the case file that identified cases for the study group.

On the Wechsler abbreviated scale of intelligence obtained full scale verbal and performance IQ in the lower half of the range associated with mild disability, that is IQ 50 to 69, that is Mother's IQ. She had difficulty in completing the block design sub test and showed a performance characterised by reversals. In another graded word reading test Mother showed an age range equivalent of 7.5 years. She was therefore defined as eligible to receive support from the Specialist Learning Disability Team from Adult Services.

Purpose of the research

The findings from research on the Assessment Framework suggest its implementation has had an impact on social work practice and inter-agency co-operation and increased the participation of parents in the assessment process (Cleaver *et al.* 2004). How far this applies to parents with a learning disability was not known. The study was commissioned by the then Department of Health to explore the assessment, process and outcomes for children in cases that involve parents with learning disabilities.

Consultation group

In order to advise the research team, a consultation group was established and met on two occasions. The purpose of the meetings was to identify changes in existing practices and procedures that would support greater co-operation in assessment, planning and interventions to best meet the needs of both the child and parents with a learning disability. The group included representatives from research, policy and practice including two major charities providing services for parents with learning disabilities. The group also included representatives from four of the participating local authorities.

Aims of the study

This study had two main aims. The first was to compare assessments for children who live with a parent with learning disabilities with children who do not and to identify factors that encourage or hinder the involvement of parents with learning disabilities in the assessment process. The second was to explore the impact of Child in Need Plans on outcomes for children living with parents with learning disabilities.

Methods

To achieve these aims the study employed the following methods:

- A study of social work case files where the parent has learning disabilities and a comparison group where parents do not.

- A qualitative study involving interviews with children over ten years of age, parents and social workers.

- A paper exercise to identify basic information on children's legal and administrative status two years after referral to children's social care.

- A follow-up study, three years after referral, of the sample of children living with parents with learning disabilities based on reviews and re-assessments held on social work case files.

- Follow-up interviews and assessments of children's progress in cases where no review or re-assessment was available on the case file or the case was closed to children's social care and children were under the age of 18 years and living with their parents. The assessment was carried out by a member of the research team in partnership with the parent using the domains and dimensions of the Assessment Framework.

The study of social work case files

The study included 76 cases where the child lived with a parent with learning disabilities (*the study group*). Cases were identified initially through an analysis of cases included in a previous study by the author (Cleaver *et al.* 2004). This brought to light 17 cases where parents had learning disabilities. The cases came from ten local authorities and included two London Boroughs, two Unitary Authorities, two Metropolitan Districts and four Shire Counties.

To increase the size of the study group six of the ten local authorities were revisited and additional cases sought and scrutinised. The following criteria were used to select cases for the sample:

- referred because of concerns about the child's safety or welfare

- one or both parents with whom the child was living had a learning disability

- the case progressed to an initial assessment or other form of assessment

- the case was referred since the implementation of the Assessment Framework and prior to August 2001.

It must be acknowledged, however, that because the research team were dependent on local authorities identifying cases this may have resulted in a degree of selective bias.

The earlier study of 2248 referrals to children's social care (Cleaver *et al.* 2004) was used to identify whether the study group exhibited significant differences in relation to the following factors:

- child's principal carer
- child's age
- child's gender
- source of referral
- reason for referral.

In order to explore the similarities and differences between cases involving a parent with learning disabilities and those that do not, a comparison group was identified from the original sample of 2248 referrals. Each case in the study group was matched with two cases where the child did not live with a parent with learning disabilities (*the comparison group*). The decision to match the study child with two comparative children was taken to ensure numbers remained robust; previous research showed that many referrals do not progress to an assessment (Cleaver *et al.* 2004). The following criteria were used to match the study child with his or her two comparators:

- reason for referral
- age group of the child
- gender of the child
- local authority responsible for the case.

This resulted in 228 referrals (76 where the child lived with a parent with learning disabilities and 152 where the child did not). Comparisons between the two groups enabled the research team to identify differences and similarities in children's needs, parenting capacity, and family and environmental factors, and the provision of services to meet identified needs.

The qualitative study

All three members of the research team have specific training and experience of working with adults with learning disabilities. Hedy Cleaver is a qualified social worker and psychologist; she has worked in training centres for adults with learning disabilities. Don Nicholson was an approved social worker under the Mental Health Act and had worked with adults with poor mental health and learning disabilities. Angela Churchill, who was involved in much of the interviewing, is currently working with adults with learning disabilities. She is a qualified social care worker and has been trained on the use of Makaton signing and symbols; she has also undertaken advanced counselling training. Police checks were carried out prior to any interviews taking place.

The 76 cases that made up the study group of referrals to children's social care represented 50 distinct families; many children lived with siblings who were also included in the study. Access to these 50 families was through the social worker who explained the research, discussed issues of confidentiality, informed the family that they could have a friend or relative present at the interview, and sought their consent to be interviewed by a member of the research team. Although the original aim had been to interview 30 families where one or more parent had learning disabilities, resource and staffing issues within children's social care meant that approaching families for research purposes was not always a priority and in a few closed cases families proved difficult to locate. As a result it was possible to gain the consent of only 23 families.

As a result the interview sample involved 23 cases where children were living with a parent with learning disabilities (*the study group*). The *comparison group* was made up of 42 cases where children were living with parents who did not have learning disabilities; these data had been collected during an earlier study by the author (Cleaver *et al.* 2004).

Interviews were carried out with the parents with learning disabilities and the social worker involved in the assessment process. By interviewing wherever possible both parents and professionals it was hoped that individual accounts, which may be shaped by their experiences, could be balanced by the views of others. The interviews were designed in a semi-structured way in order, as far as possible, to mirror normal social interactions (Burgess 1984; Hammersley and Atkinson 1983).

INTERVIEWS WITH PARENTS

It was particularly important to ensure parents with learning disabilities were as relaxed and feeling as confident and in control as possible. One way of lowering anxiety is to carry out the interview within the parents' own home. In all but two cases this was possible; at the request of the parent one mother was interviewed in her friend's house, and in the other case the interview was conducted at the children's social care office.

Taking part in an interview can be bewildering and stressful for some parents with learning disabilities. To counteract this, parents were reassured they could have a relative, friend or worker present during the interview. In ten cases (43%) the parent with learning disabilities was supported in some way during the research interview. In three cases a professional (social worker or care worker) introduced the researcher to the mother and reassured her that she could ask for her help whenever she wanted, and then remained in the house during the interview, although not in the room where the interview took place. One interview took place at a children's social care office and again the social worker made the introductions and offered on-going help. In a further three cases the interview took place in the parent's home and a member of the family or family friend was present. Finally, in three cases both parents were interviewed together in their home. In the remaining 13 cases the parent with learning disabilities was unsupported during the interview.

Interviews with parents covered the following issues and took anywhere from one to two hours depending on the parent:

- the reason for contact with children's social care
- parents' understanding of the reason and purpose of the assessment
- parental involvement and participation in the assessment process
- the adequacy of the assessment – did it cover all the issues they believed were relevant?

In the study group 14 (60.9%) interviews were carried out with a lone mother, in 6 (26.1%) cases a lone father, and in 3 (13%) cases both parents were interviewed. In the comparison group children were living with a greater diversity of female carers, but male carers featured less frequently. Interviews were done with 38 (90.4%) lone female carers (36 mothers, one grandmother, and one great aunt). In one case a lone stepfather was interviewed, and in two cases the child's mother and her partner were interviewed.

Interviewing young people who were living with a parent with learning disabilities proved difficult because in only five cases was the child over the age of ten years, and in three of these cases the young person had learning difficulties. The results from the interviews carried out with the remaining two young people have not been included in the study.

INTERVIEWS WITH SOCIAL WORKERS

In every case the social worker was interviewed. Interviews were conducted at a time and place convenient to the worker. The interview covered the following issues:

- the circumstances surrounding the referral
- what was done to prepare the family for the assessment
- how the assessment was carried out, including issues such as involving the family, working with other agencies, and working within the required time-frame.

The interview schedules for parents and social workers were the same as those used in a previous study undertaken by the author in order that the findings from cases involving parents with learning disabilities could be compared with the findings from those that did not (Cleaver *et al.* 2004).

A study of legal and administrative outcomes

Information on the legal and administrative outcomes for children and families during the two years following the assessment was sought on the study group and half the comparison group. Local authorities were able to provide these data on 62 cases in the study group and 59 in the comparison group. This information was sought from the link person in each participating local authority. The initial request included information about the services that had been provided to the families by both 'children and family services' and 'adult services', since the assessment. However, it quickly become apparent that staff in children's services could not readily provide information about services provided by adult services.

To enable information to be easily accessed by managers or administrative staff the data were restricted to information that was expected to be recorded electronically. Such electronically recorded information included the child's legal status, whether the case was open, if the child's name was on the child protection register, whether children's social care were providing a service to the child, and whether services were being provided to the parent with learning disabilities.

The response from the participating local authorities varied considerably. Although some were able to access the information from a central electronic system, this was not always straightforward and in one authority the task proved so complicated that it required the assistance of an experienced IT operator. In most local authorities at the time of the study the information was not available centrally or electronically and managers had to request social workers to access the information manually. This was a time-consuming process and resulted in less reliable data. For example, in some cases it was reported that the information was no longer available, either because the case had been closed or the family had moved out of the area. In either scenario the authority should have retained some information. In other cases it was known that the files were in specific offices but the local workers did not respond to the request for information. Finally, in a few cases it was reported that the cases did not exist. This was difficult to understand, as only cases that had been studied were included in the request for additional administrative information. These reasons accounted for 14 cases where no follow-up data were accessible and in a further 17 cases the case number had not been available to the researcher at the time the file was studied, and no follow-up was possible.

The follow-up study of children living with a parent with learning disabilities

To identify children for the follow-up study the case numbers for children of the original study group were sent to the link person in each of the participating local authorities. Once cases had been located arrangements were made for a member of the research team to scrutinise each case file.

In 12 cases no follow-up was possible. In ten instances the case numbers for children who were living with parents with learning disabilities had not been available to the research team when the initial case file study was being carried out. In a further two cases changes to the local authorities' recording systems had made follow-up impossible.

A comparison of the cases included in the follow-up with those where no follow-up information was available shows few differences. For example, the proportion of children referred because of child protection concerns was very similar; 43.7 per cent in the follow-up sample compared with 41.7 per cent of cases in the group where no follow-up was possible. Moreover, gender was not relevant: boys accounted for 60.9 per cent of the follow-up sample and 66.6 per cent of the remaining cases. The only real differences related to the age of the children; the cases where no follow-up had been possible included a disproportionate number of young people aged 10–14 years at the time of referral. Half the 12 children where no follow-up was possible fell within this age group compared with only 17 per cent of cases that were followed up.

The exploration of children's progress and circumstances focused on those children who continued to live with a parent with learning disabilities. Cases were included in the follow-up study when they fitted the following criteria:

- the child lived continuously with his or her parents since first assessment
- the child had lived part-time with his or her parents since first assessment (i.e. those who had experienced short-term foster care or residential care or hospital care)
- the child had become looked after during 2004 (the year that the follow-up study was undertaken).

Children were to be excluded when they had:

- been adopted
- lived away from home continuously
- been continuously looked after for the past 12 months.

Fifty-two children fitted these criteria. However, there was further attrition to the data set because no assessment following the referral was found on the case file for seven children. Exploring the extent to which services met identified needs was therefore confined to 45 cases.

Exploring the progress of children who continued to live with parents with learning disabilities was by definition confined to cases where there were both baseline and current data. When case files did not contain a current assessment or review of children's progress, attempts were made to contact the parent in order to carry out an assessment of the child based on the domains and dimensions of the Assessment Framework.

In cases that were open to children's social care or had only recently been closed, the relevant social worker made the initial approach to the family. Local authorities used a variety of methods to contact parents dependent on the family circumstances, including letters, telephone calls and home visits. On approaching families social workers explained or reminded parents of the research, reiterated issues of confidentiality, encouraged parents to have a friend or relative present if they wished, and sought their consent for a member of the research team to approach them.

For closed cases that were not known to any current worker, a professional member of the headquarters staff sent a letter to the last known address, giving some brief information about the research and asking if a member of the research team could contact them. With families already known to the research team (they had been involved in the first round of interviews) a letter, telephone call or home visit was made by a member of the team to seek their continued involvement in the study.

Gaining access to families proved difficult, and it was only possible to gather information, either from the case file or through carrying out an assessment, on the progress of 36 children. The group was further restricted because in five cases no baseline data were available.

Cases fell by the wayside for a number of reasons. In five cases families either withdrew or social workers asked us not to make contact; in two cases families did not wish to be included in the second stage of the research; and in a further three the social worker felt it was inappropriate to contact the family as the case was at a very sensitive point.

In 12 cases social workers failed to make contact with the parents; letters were returned by the post office with the following comments: 'gone away, letter returned unopened as addressee not collected from post office', or simply 'left'. Attempts by social workers to contact families directly by telephone or home visits were also not always successful. Similar results were found when a member of the research team tried to reconnect with families. Speculative visits frequently resulted in finding derelict and unoccupied houses. In some cases local authorities were aware that the family had moved but had no new address. Approaches made to adult services and the health visiting service to help identify the family's current address resulted in identifying the whereabouts of only one family.

In all cases where parents agreed to take part in the study, a member of the research team explained issues of confidentiality and sought their consent to talk to their child. Parents were encouraged to ask questions about the study and assured that they were under no obligation to participate. When parents agreed, an assessment of the child's progress, using the domains and dimensions of the Assessment Framework, was undertaken in partnership with them; whenever possible children also contributed to the assessment. All members of the research team are familiar with principles and research underpinning the Assessment Framework and have considerable experience in using it.

Managing the data

The data gathered from the study of social work case files and the interviews with parents and social workers were subjected to both quantitative and qualitative analysis. The data set from previous research by the author (Cleaver *et al.* 2004) was used to identify differences in the overall profile of cases that involved children living with a parent with learning disabilities. This original data set was also used to identify a comparison group, matched with regard to the reason for referral, age and gender of the child, and the local authority responsible for the case. The data from the study of social work case files was analysed using SPSS (Statistical Package for the Social Sciences). The size of the sample allowed tests of significance to be applied.

The interview study included 23 cases where children were living with a parent with learning disabilities. The interview schedule used in the author's previous study enabled comparisons to be made with the findings from that study (Cleaver *et al.* 2004). Because the numbers were small, no sophisticated statistics have been applied to these findings. Qualitative methods were applied to the data to identify meaningful themes that represent the experiences of parents and social workers. The findings were used in a descriptive manner to aid the understanding and interpretation of the data from the study of social work case files.

The data from the follow-up study were also analysed using a variety of methods. For example, the data on children's progress were assessed with the help of a statistical package (SPSS). In contrast, qualitative methods were used to explore the stories recounted by parents and the information recorded on social work files in order to contextualise these findings and identify underlying factors and important themes.

Tables

Table A.1 Child's principal carer				
Study	Mother	Father	Other	Total in sample[1]
Study group	81.7%	16.9%	1.4%	71
All referrals	83.7%	13.0%	3.3%	1634

1   Information on the identity of the principal carer had not been recorded in every case.

Table A.2 Source of the referral			
Study	Professional sources	Non-professional sources	Total in sample[1]
Study group	89.7%	10.3%	68
All referrals	70.5%	29.5%	2168

1   Information on the source of the referral had not been recorded in every case.

Table A.3 Main reason for the initial assessment

Reason for initial assessment[1]	Study group	Comparison group
Child protection concerns	23 (42.6%)	35 (48.6%)
Parental learning disability	9 (16.7%)	0
Other parenting issues	14 (25.9%)	12 (16.7%)
Parental mental illness/substance misuse/domestic violence	4 (7.4%)	14 (19.4%)
Disabled child	3 (5.6%)	2 (2.8%)
Child /young person beyond parental control	1 (1.9%)	6 (8.3%)
Other	0	3 (4.2%)
Total	54 (100%)	72 (100%)

1   The reason for the initial assessment had not been recorded on the case file in two
     study cases and one case in the comparison group.

Table A.4 The rate of unmet developmental needs identified by the social workers' initial assessment

Study	Health	Educa-tion	Emotional and behavioural development	Identity and social development	Family and social relation-ships
Study group n=56	30 (61.2%)	28 (60.9%)	25 (54.3%)	20 (44.4%)	39 (79.6%)
Comparison group n=76	23 (36.5%)	27 (43.5%)	19 (30.2%)	16 (25.8%)	37 (56.9%)
Total	53 (47.3%)	55 (50.9%)	44 (40.4%)	36 (33.6%)	76 (66.7%)

Note: Social work recording was not always consistent. For the study group, information was missing in the following dimensions: health and family and social relationships – seven cases, education and emotional and behavioural development – ten cases, identity and social development – 11 cases. In the comparison group the following information was missing: 13 cases in relation to health and emotional and behavioural development, 14 cases in relation to education and identity and social development, and 11 cases in relation to family and social relationships. The following differences were found to be statistically significant:
Health – Pearson Chi-square 6.755 (1) <0.009.
Emotional and behavioural development – Pearson Chi-square 6.462 (1) <0.011.
Family and social relationships – Pearson Chi-square 6.461 (1) <0.011.

Table A.5 The rate of difficulties in parenting capacity identified by the social workers' initial assessment

Study	Basic care	Ensuring safety	Emo-tional warmth	Stimu-lation	Guidance and bound-aries	Stabil-ity
Study group n=56	27 (54.0%)	29 (58.0%)	10 (20.4%)	27 (56.3%)	32 (68.1%)	23 (47.9%)
Comparison group n=76	12 (19.0%)	23 (36.5%)	8 (13.1%)	7 (12.5%)	18 (30.0%)	22 (36.7%)
Total	39 (34.5%)	52 (46.0%)	18 (16.4%)	34 (32.7%)	50 (46.7%)	45 (41.7%)

Note: Social work recording was not always consistent. For the study group, information was missing in the following dimensions: in both basic care and ensuring safety – six cases, emotional warmth – seven cases, both stimulation and stability – eight cases, guidance and boundaries – nine cases. In the comparison group the following information was missing: 13 cases each in relation to basic care and ensuring safety, 15 cases in relation to emotional warmth, 16 cases in relation to guidance and boundaries and stability, and 20 cases in relation to stimulation. The following differences were found to be statistically significant:
Basic care – Pearson Chi-square 15.068 (1) <0.000.
Stimulation – Pearson Chi-square 22.482 (1) <0.000.
Guidance and boundaries – Pearson Chi-square 15.457 (1) <0.000.

Table A.6 The rate of difficulties within the family and environmental domain identified by the social workers' initial assessment

Study	Family history and functioning	Social resources	Housing	Employment
Study group n=56	42 (89.4%)	34 (68.0%)	22 (44.0%)	27 (56.3%)
Comparison group n=76	42 (64.0%)	30 (48.4%)	10 (16.4%)	21 (35.0%)
Total	84 (78.5%)	64 (57.1%)	32 (28.8%)	48 (44.4%)

Note: Social work recording was not always consistent. For the study group, information was missing in the following dimensions: in family history and functioning – nine cases, both social resources and housing – six cases, and employment – eight cases. In the comparison group the following information was missing: 16 cases in relation to family history and functioning, 15 cases in relation to housing, 14 cases in relation to social resources, and 13 cases in relation to employment. The following difference was found to be statistically significant:

Housing – Pearson Chi-square 10.206 (1) <0.001.

Table A.7 A comparison of the rate of children's developmental needs identified by the social workers' core assessment

Developmental dimension	Study group n=26 Children over 5 years n=16	Comparison group n=14 Children over 5 years n=8	Previous research by the author[1] n=41 Children over 5 years n=22
Health	20 (76.9%)	10 (71.4%)	26 (63.4%)
Education	20 (76.9%)	10 (71.4%)	26 (65.0%)
Emotional and behavioural development	21 (80.8%)	8 (57.1%)	28 (68.3%)
Identity	15 (57.7%)	7 (50%)	22 (62.9%)
Family and social relationships	20 (76.9%)	7 (50%)	25 (67.6%)

Table A.7 *cont.*

Developmental dimension	Study group n=26 Children over 5 years n=16	Comparison group n=14 Children over 5 years n=8	Previous research by the author[1] n=41 Children over 5 years n=22
Social presentation (not applicable to child under five years)	10 (62.5%)	2 (25%)	17 (77.3%)
Selfcare skills (not applicable to child under five years)	9 (56.3%)	2 (25%)	16 (72.7%)

1   Cleaver and Walker with Meadows (2004). Forty-one children of whom 22 were aged over 5 years. Information not recorded on every case: one case missing for education, six for identity and four for family and social relationships.

Table A.8 Cases open to children and family services			
Study	Case open	Case closed	Total
Study group	38 (62.3%)	23 (37.7%)	61 (100%)
Comparison group	13 (22.0%)	46 (78.0%)	59 (100%)
Total	51 (42.5%)	69 (57.5%)	120 (100%)

Note: Difference found to be statistically significant – Pearson Chi-square 19.894 (1) <0.000.

Table A.9 Services provided to meet parents' needs			
Study	Services provided for parent	No services provided for parent	Total
Study group	33 (67.3%)	16 (32.7%)	49 (100%)
Comparison group	11 (40.7%)	16 (59.3%)	27 (100%)
Total	44 (57.9%)	32 (42.1%)	76 (100%)

Note: Information on whether parents were receiving a service to meet their own needs was only available in 76 cases. Difference found to be statistically significant – Pearson Chi-square 5.632 (1) <0.025.

Table A.10 Children's names registered on the child protection register			
Study	Child on the CPR	Child not on the CPR	Total
Study group	16 (25.8%)	46 (74.2%)	62 (100%)
Comparison group	2 (3.4%)	57 (96.6%)	59 (100%)
Total	18 (14.9%)	103 (85.1%)	121 (100%)

Note: Difference found to be statistically significant – Pearson Chi-square 11.997 (1) <0.001.

References

Booth, T. and Booth, W. (1996) *Parenting under Pressure: Mothers and Fathers with Learning Difficulties.* Buckingham: Open University Press.

Burgess, R.G. (1984) *The Research Process in Educational Settings.* Lewis: Falmer.

CHANGE (2005) *Report of National Gathering of Parents with Learning Disabilities.* Leeds: CHANGE.

Cleaver, H. and Freeman, P. (1995) *Parental Perspectives in Cases of Suspected Child Abuse.* London: HMSO.

Cleaver, H. and Freeman, P. (1996) 'Child Abuse which Involves Wider Kin and Family Friends.' In P. Bibby (ed.) *Organised Abuse: The Current Debate.* London: Arena.

Cleaver, H., Unell, I. and Aldgate, J. (1999) Children's Needs – Parenting Capacity: The Impact of Parental Mental Illness, Problem Alcohol and Drug Use, and Domestic Violence on Children's Development. London: The Stationary Office.

Cleaver, H. and Walker, S. with Meadows, P. (2004) *Assessing Children's Needs and Circumstances: The Impact of the Assessment Framework.* London: Jessica Kingsley Publishers.

Cm 5086 (2001) *Valuing People: A New Strategy for Learning Disability for the 21st Century.* London: The Stationery Office.

Cm 5860 (2003) *Every Child Matters.* London: The Stationery Office.

Cm 6449 (2005) *Independence, Well-being and Choice: Our vision for the future of social care for adults in England.* Norwich: The Stationery Office.

Commission for Social Care Inspection, HM Inspectorate of Court Administration, the Healthcare Commission, HM Inspectorate of Constabulary, HM Inspectorate of Probation, HM Inspectorate of Prisons, HM Crown Prosecution Service Inspectorate and the Office for Standards in Education (2005) *The Second Chief Inspectors' Report on Arrangements to Safeguard Children.* www.safeguardingchildren.org.uk, accessed on 22 October 2007.

Community Care (2006) *Interview with New Learning Difficulties Tsar, Nicola Smith.* www.communitycare.co.uk/searchservices/search.aspx?searchtype=site&skeywords=interview+with+new+learninganddisability+tsar, accessed on 10 October 2007.

Cope, C. (2003) *Fulfilling Lives: Inspection of Social Care Services for People with Learning Disabilities.* London: Social Services Inspectorate, Department of Health.

Cotson, D., Friend, J., Hollins, S. and James, H. (2001) 'Implementing the Framework for the Assessment of Children in Need and their Families when the Parent has a Learning Disability.' In J. Horwath (ed.) *The Child's World.* London: Jessica Kingsley Publishers.

Dearden, C. and Becker, S. (2002) *Young Carers and Education.* London: Carers UK.

Department for Education and Skills (2006) *About the Integrated Children's System.* London: Department for Education and Skills. www.everychildmatters.gov.uk/ICS/about/uk/search/?asset=document&id=2866, accesssed on 10 October 2007.

Department of Health (2000) *Framework for the Assessment of Children in Need and their Families, Guidance Notes and Glossary for: Referral and Initial Information Record, Initial Assessment Record and Core Assessment Record.* London: The Stationery Office.

Department of Health (2002) *Integrated Children's System: Working with Children in Need and their Families, Consultation Document.* London: DOH. www.everychildmatters.gov.uk/socialcare, accessed on 10 October 2007.

Department of Health and Cleaver, H. (2000) *Assessment Recording Forms.* London: The Stationery Office.

Department of Health, Cox, A. and Bentovim, A. (2000b) *Framework for the Assessment of Children in Need and their Families, The Family Pack of Questionnaires and Scales.* London: The Stationery Office.

Department of Health, Department for Education and Employment, Home Office (2000a) *Framework for the Assessment of Children in Need and their Families.* London: The Stationery Office.

Department of Health and Department for Education and Skills (2004) *National Service Framework for Children, Young People and Maternity Services.* London: Department of Health.

Dowdney, L. and Skuse, D. (1993) 'Parenting provided by adults with mental retardation.' *Journal of Child Psychology and Psychiatry 34,* 1, 25–47.

Emerson, E., Malam, S., Davies, I. and Spencer, K. (2005) *Adults with Learning Disabilities in England 2003/4.* Leeds: Health and Social Care Information Centre.

Feldman, M.A., Varghese, J., Ramsay, J. and Rajska, D. (2002) 'Relationships between social support, stress and mother–child interactions in mothers with intellectual disabilities.' *Journal of Applied Research in Intellectual Disabilities 15,* 314–323.

Ghate, D. and Hazel, N. (2002) *Parenting in Poor Environments: Stress, Support and Coping.* London: Jessica Kingsley Publishers.

Goodinge, S. (2000) *A Jigsaw of Services: Inspection of Services to Support Disabled Adults in their Parenting Role.* London: Department of Health.

Hammersley, M. and Atkinson, P. (1983) *Ethnography: Principles in Practice.* London: Tavistock.

HM Government (2004) *Every Child Matters: Change for Children.* London: Department for Education and Skills.

HM Government (2006a) *Working Together to Safeguard Children: A Guide to Inter-agency Working to Safeguard and Promote the Welfare of Children.* London: The Stationery Office.

HM Government (2006b) *Making Safeguarding Everyone's Business: The Government's Response to the Second Chief Inspector's Report on Arrangements to Safeguard Children.* www.everychildmatters.gov.uk/resources_and_practice/IG00045, accessed on 10 October 2007.

HM Government (2006c) *What to Do if You're Worried a Child is Being Abused.* London: Department for Education and Skills.

Hopkins, L. (2002) *Daventry Family Centre: Parenting Skills Group.* Daventry: NCH.

McConnell, D. and Llewellyn, G. (2000) 'Disability and discrimination in statutory child protection proceedings.' *Disability and Society 15,* 6, 883–895.

McConnell, D. and Llewellyn, G. (2002) 'Stereotypes, parents with intellectual disability and child protection.' *Journal of Social Welfare and Family Law 24*, 3, 296–317.

McGaw, S. (1996) 'Services for parents with learning disabilities.' *Learning Disability Review 1*, 1, 21–32.

McGaw, S. (2000) *What Works for Parents with Learning Disabilities.* Essex: Barnardo's.

McGaw, S., Beckley, K., Connolly, N. and Ball, K. (1999) *Parenting Assessment Manual.* Cornwall & Isle of Scilly Health Authority: Special Parenting Service.

McGaw, S. and Newman, T. (2005) *What Works for Parents with Learning Disabilities?* Essex: Barnardo's.

McGaw, S. and Sturmey, P. (1993) 'Identifying the needs of parents with learning disabilities: a review.' *Child Abuse Review 2*, 101–117.

McGaw, S. and Sturmey, P. (1994) 'Assessing parents with learning disabilities: the parent skills model.' *Child Abuse Review 3*, 36–51.

Mackinnon, S., Bailey, B. and Pink, L. (2004) *Understanding Learning Disabilities: A Video-based Training Resource for Trainers and Managers to Use with Their Staff.* Brighton: Pavilion.

Morris, J. (2003) *The Right Support: Report of the Task Force on Supporting Disabled Adults in their Parenting Role.* York: Joseph Rowntree Foundation.

Morris, J. (2004) *Disabled Parents and Schools: Barriers to Parental Involvement in Children's Education.* York: Joseph Rowntree Foundation.

NSPCC and The University of Sheffield (2000) *The Child's World: Assessing Children in Need. Training and Development Pack.* London: NSPCC.

Rende, R. and Plomin, R. (1993) 'Families at risk from psychopathology: who becomes at risk and why?' *Development and Psychopathology 5*, 4, 529–540.

Schilling, R., Schinke, S., Blythe, B. and Barth, R. (1982) 'Child maltreatment and mentally retarded parents: is there a relationship?' *Mental Retardation 20*, 5, 201–209.

SCIE (2005) *The Health and Well-being of Young Carers: Research Briefing 11.* www.scie.org.uk/publications/briefings/briefing11/index.asp, accessed on 10 October 2007.

Seagull, E.A.W. and Scheurer, S.L. (1986) 'Neglected and abused children of mentally retarded parents.' *Child Abuse and Neglect 10*, 493–500.

Social Services Inspectorate, Commission for Health Improvement, HM Inspectorate of Constabulary, HM Crown Prosecution Service Inspectorate, HM Magistrates Courts' Inspectorate, Ofsted, HM Inspectorate of Prisons, HM Inspectorate of Probation (2002) *Safeguarding Children: A Joint Chief Inspectors' Report on the Arrangements to Safeguard Children.* London: Department of Health.

Tarleton, B., Ward, L. and Howarth, J. (2006) 'Finding the Right Support? A Review of Issues and Positive Practice in Supporting Parents with Learning Difficulties and their Children.' *Health and Social Care in the Community 15*, 1, 95–96.

Terman, L. and Merrill, M.A. (1960) *Stanford Binet Intelligence Scale.* Boston, MA: Houghton Mifflin.

Tymchuck, A. (1992) 'Predicting adequacy of parenting by people with mental retardation.' *Child Abuse and Neglect 16*, 165–178.

Tymchuck, A. and Andron, L. (1990) 'Mothers with mental retardation who do or do not abuse or neglect their children.' *Child Abuse and Neglect 14*, 313–323.

Ward, H., Munroe, E.R. and Dearden, C. (2006) *Babies and Young Children in Care: Life Pathways, Decision-making and Practice.* London: Jessica Kingsley Publishers.

Wates, M. (2002) *Supporting Disabled Adults in their Parenting Role.* York: York Publishing Services.

Wechsler, D. (1974) *Wechsler Adult Intelligence Scale – Revised.* New York, NY: Psychological Corporation.

Weir, A. (2003) 'A Framework for Assessing Parents with Mental Health Problems.' In M.C. Calder and S. Hackett (eds) *Assessment in Child Care.* Dorset: Russell House.

Subject Index

Author Index